EMBODIMENT

HOW ANIMALS AND HUMANS MAKE SENSE OF THINGS:

THE DAWN OF ART, ETHICS, SCIENCE, POLITICS, AND RELIGION

2020 EDITION

JESSE JAMES THOMAS

Embodiment
How Animals and Humans Make Sense of Things:
The Dawn of Art, Ethics, Science, Politics, and Religion
Copyright © 2020 by Jesse James Thomas

Library of Congress Control Number: 9781647492243
ISBN-13: Paperback: 978-1-64749-224-3
        Hardback: 978-1-64749-230-4
        Epub: 978-1-64749-225-0

All rights reserved. No part of this publication may be reproduced, distributed, or transmitted in any form or by any means, including photocopying, recording, or other electronic or mechanical methods, without the prior written permission of the publisher or author, except in the case of brief quotations embodied in critical reviews and certain other noncommercial uses permitted by copyright law.

Although every precaution has been taken to verify the accuracy of the information contained herein, the author and publisher assume no responsibility for any errors or omissions.No liability is assumed for damages that may result from the use of information contained within.

Printed in the United States of America

GoToPublish LLC
1-888-337-1724
www.gotopublish.com
info@gotopublish.com

Reviews of First Edition in 2018 of *Embodiment, How Animals and Humans Make Sense of Things* **from a wide variety of readers.**

CHRISTINE MULLIGAN
Thomas Mulligan Music Promotions

I do not frequently marvel at the avenues down which humanity has driven itself – especially within the last 3 decades or so. I do appreciate and value the message and narrative of the informative, insightful and entertaining. As does Dr. Thomas, I respect and try to learn from the world around me – at large, and in my own backyard. I often marvel at the innate abilities and knowledge of its non-human inhabitants and wonder if we humans have lost all touch with such valuable instincts. Embodiment incorporates Dr. Thomas's own amusing encounters with animals, illustrating their instincts (including the humans they encounter!). He also walks us through the ethical developments of characters in current films such as Meet Joe Black and several James Bond movies. His final "Scene" brings us an inclusive discussion of "Embodied Religion" – an open-ended conversation with universal appeal.

Dr. Thomas's style reveals both his brilliant intellect and his earthy, basic understanding of the world around him. His easy manner is most appealing, and his knowledge seems immeasurable. For someone so cerebral, he sounds like a lovely "Mayberry" type of guy.

***** 5 Amazon Review Stars

ARTHUR WILLIAM RAYBOLD
Author of *Home From The Banks*

Jesse Thomas delightfully disarms us by recording meticulously how his bats, bees, raccoons, pigs, geese, and bears make sense of things while improving their species. This once Indiana experiential education guides us through biology, psychology and Gestalt therapy by employing four films whose characters feel and act on empathy, sympathy and compassion to make sense of their lives. I would suggest that Embodiment be required for a high school diploma along with the swimming certificate.

***** 5 Amazon Review Stars

RICK GRIHALVA
Businessman Owner, *Forever in Stiches Quilts*

Every morning the local farmers come into our local McDonalds, have coffee, breakfast, and talk. When I read Dr. Jesse James Thomas Embodiment it felt like I was sitting down talking with them, which I sometimes do, even though I am not a farmer or a "dirt stick" farmer type, as Jesse Thomas sometimes describes himself. Reading his book is like sitting in with him at McDonalds or perhaps in his "Jungle" back yard, just talking about life and earlier times in our lives. Jesse's writing departs from an earlier book of his that I read. This one is humorous, conversational, and thought provoking in a most non-confrontational way with me, the reader.

***** 5 Amazon Review Stars

JAYAKUMAR RAGHAVAN
Author of *Science for Living, Five Science Topics for Religion and Society*

It "came to me" that I should read this book, because I have occasionally felt deep connections with animals when I visited zoos or watched backyard birds. (Not so much with household pets). I have also laughed at people who comment that gorillas and chimpanzees act so much like people and said, No it is we who act like them. So as I read this delightful book studded with scientific facts, entertaining stories and folk wisdom, I realize that the author is providing us sustenance at this "Shiawassee Flats", while we are on our way to learning when we go where we want to go.

This book thrills us with unexpected associations and verified corrections between empathy, compassion, philosophy, neurology, and simple life lessons, with playful linguistic usages. The author subtly points out that the celebrated intuition or instinct are what animals have always had and we might achieve greater successes if we didn't resist "wallowing with the pigs". As a follower of the science of complex and dynamic systems (Chaos), I find characteristics and consequences of such systems casually illustrated by this accessible book. The book is a "must read" for everyone, lay people and specialists.

***** 5 Amazon Review stars

CONTENTS

DEDICATION vii
Important Preface ix
INTRODUCTION xi

PART 1

WHAT COMES TO US *MEET JOE BLACK*
SCENE 1 PIGS: MAKING SENSE OF THINGS 11
SCENE 2 CHICKENS AND THEIR EGGS:
GETTING OFF TO A GOODSTART 18
SCENE 3 CANADIAN GEESE: WHERE TO GONEXT 26
SCENE 4 BATS: SENSING THE SURROUNDINGS 33
SCENE 5 BEARS: TRIAL AND ERROR 40
SCENE 6 RACCOONS: COPING SKILLS 46
SCENE 7 HONEYBEES: COMMUNITY LIFE 53

PART 2

INSTINCT *SPECTRE* *61*
PART 2 SCENE 1 FROM EMPATHY TO COMPASSION 71
PART 2 SCENE 2 THE NEUROLOGY OF EMOTION 77
PART 2 SCENE 3 INTENTIONAL GOALS 83
PART 2 SCENE 4 UTILIZING OPTIONS 91
PART 2 SCENE 5 THE DYNAMICS OF TINKERING 97
PART 2 SCENE 6 FROM NOVICE TOEXPERT 104
PART 2 SCENE 7 HUMAN CULTURE 111

PART 3

THE DAWNING OF EMBODIED CULTURE *TEARS OF THE SUN* *121*
PART 3 SCENE 1 EMBODIED ART 130
PART 3 SCENE 2 EMBODIED ETHICS 138
SCENE 3 EMBODIED SCIENCE 144
PART 3 SCENE 4 THE BODY POLITIC 150
PART 3 SCENE 5 EMBODIEDRELIGION 157

PART 4

APPLICATIONS IN EMBODIED LIFE *THE EDGE OF TOMORROW* *169*
PART 4 SCENE 1 ARTISTIC APPLICATIONS: THE PREGNANCY OF ART 172
PART 4 SCENE 2 ETHICAL APPLICATIONS: CHILDHOOD ETHICS 178
PART 4 SCENE 3 SCIENCE APPLICATIONS: NATURE AND ANIMALS AS SCIENTISTS 184
PART 4 SCENE 4 POLITICAL APPLICATIONS: POLITICAL SURVIVAL IN THE 21ST CENTURY 190
PART 4 SCENE 5 RELIGIOUS APPLICATIONS: LIFE IS MORE THAN TIME OR SPACE CAN TEACH US. 197
EPILOGUE 205
DAWN 206
RECOMMENDED BOOKS 207

DEDICATION

To my four wonderful daughters,
whom I love and adore:

Carla
Claudia
Lisa
Jessica

IMPORTANT PREFACE

This book is about how animals make sense of things, and how understanding this helps human make better sense of things too in everyday life. Please slow down a bit while reading this book. Don't jump to the end to see who robbed the bank or killed the hero's mother.

There is an obsession today with doing everything as fast as possible. Speed-reading and fast-talking may have some advantages, but not in this book. Besides, living that way can make your life speed by so quickly it will be next year before you know it, then the next year after that, etc.

Research shows that students taking notes quickly on a laptop may get a more detailed record of what the teacher said, but *comprehend* it less than those taking notes by hand. There is no rote memory exam after reading this book.

This book is to help you teach yourself, OK? So slow down; get in touch with what *Makes Sense* to *you*. Detailed and coded learning "packages" can sometimes work, but not if *you* have difficulty fitting yourself into a *package*. What this book is trying to teach doesn't *package* easily. Can you groove to that?

This book is *unpacked* one paragraph at a time, Each paragraph is meant to feed forward and occasionally back to earlier paragraphs.

Meanwhile I'll do my best to make the book readable, entertaining, and practical.

Editors of my articles for science and academic journals mean well, but in the cause of "objectivity" (packages) they usually discourage using personal pronouns. This book is full of them in an effort to make it as conversational as possible.

Capital letters, bold type, and italics are not used according to standard texts but as an effort to make the book read as conversational. There are also no footnotes or direct quotes, only general references to Recommended Books at the end.

So feed your cat, dog, canary, goldfish, or whoever. Take off your shoes. Make yourself comfortable. You can even read parts of it aloud to your pet, especially the animal sections of Part 1. Put on some good music if that works for you. Connecting sight and sound is usually a good idea, however you do it.

If your cat starts to purr, it is a good sign. If you do, that is ok too because you have probably been working too hard lately. You can al- ways start reading again whenever you are up for it.

INTRODUCTION

Embodiment 2020 Edition, like the *Youniverse* 2020 Edition, is designed not for the usual academic but a broader public audience and acts accordingly. Anyone who has read *Youniverse* knows I utilize Bottom-Up rather than Top-Down approaches.

Top-down documents and/or fixed beliefs may be ok, but only if it is your personal cup of tea. I build upward from the bare roots of Nature in this book. This may take more time, but *it can produce deeper Results*.

We humans actually pick up where animals leave off in developing our own Survival Strategies in today's Chaotic Cultural Complexities.

This book is not primarily about detailed information and theory, although it does include some. Instead, in Parts 1 and 2 especially concern how I learned things Experientially from animals. The entire book, as in *Youniverse*, is full of anecdotal stories demonstrating parallels in animals and humans. If you have read *Youniverse*, you know stories are often more convincing than numbers.

In them the animals, not me, are the heroes. As you will see all through the book, *I usually play the role of a stage-hand who just works here, not a hero*. It is often clear that animals, despite their limitations, are wiser than many *Polarized Humans today who claim radical differences between Feelings and Thinking and usually discount the former. To animals they are always inevitably linked.* (More about Polarization later.)

This book is therefore an Emotional Book about Emotions, meaning Motivations that Move us both physically and mentally as we *Emerge* individually and socially in our lives. *Evolutionary Motivation characterizes everybody from single-celled life through animals to us.*

Life is always a matter of Motivation *and* Learning. Evolutionary Learning can require hundreds of generations. For us humans this can happen sometimes within a single lifetime. Have you personally learned much since you were born? Of course you have.

This book concerns what animals can teach us about our Emotions, all the way into our Cultural Orientation.

Animals in this book mean any creature who is *Mobile* or *Animated* (we don't call them *Animals* for nothing) found in North America, including insects.

All four Parts deal with the *Embodiment* of *Emotion* within us. Parts 1 and 2 are not about how animals are similar to us, but how we are similar to animals, far more than you may think. Animals in Parts 1 and 2 provide groundwork for Parts 3 and 4, both of which move from Individual to Cultural issues focusing on today's Embodied Art, Ethics, Science, Politics, and Religion.

Embodiment suggests that Learning begins and never leaves the Whole Body the way it often does today in Disembodied Minds. Embodiment refers to the highly specialized psychological science today called *Embodied Cognitive Science*. More about this later, so please *Bear* with me.

C. S. Peirce (pronounced "Purse") over a century ago was the great American scientist/philosopher who created *Pragmatism and among other things a different interpretation of Evolution* from that of Charles

Darwin. He also fits well with recent *Complex Systems Theory*. Other persons and terms will be added as we go along.

This book focuses especially on the *Creative Edge of Embodiment*, beginning in Part 1 with "What Comes to Us" Spontaneously and Creatively. Creativity *may* occur during Conscious Reflection, but in this book the emphasis is on what arises Spontaneously, *not* from Formulas of Reflection. Animals are creative but don't think *about* things much if ever, *nor do we every time something new "comes to us"*.

Since we humans have forgotten so much of this, they will be our teachers, helping us to understand Life in general. Meanwhile animals can occasionally offer as much help in understanding movies as movie critics.

I follow the model of down-home teachers I have known: *You don't tell folks what to think, you talk in terms they can not only understand but find useful in their lives.*

With that in mind, I will try to explain in terms of *everyday experience* such things as *Complex Systems Theory, Embodied Cognitive Science*, and other terms you may have heard of but not understood all that well, like *Pragmatism* and *Evolution*. And beyond that are new ways to understand your own Experiential development.

The first two italicized terms in the last paragraph are often described as beautiful theories that get so lost in such fancy language that even academic types cannot understand them. This little book will attempt to show you the difference they make in your Experience, not just your Ideas.

Beautiful theories can be useful every day you get up or later walk out the door. You have heard often of Pragmatism and Evolution but still not understood them well. So please be patient. Don't jump ahead in the book or you won't really learn much, as noted in the Preface.

Just wait and see. As my farmer friends from childhood would ask: "What more could you want, egg in your beer?" (We will talk about farmers and eggs in Part 1, Scene 2.)

What follows now is an effort to establish my credibility. If you don't need that, skip it and go directly to Part 1, but it is very relevant to the book.

Where I come *from* (dangling prepositions are explained later), neither side of my family were farmers, but my parents grew up next door to each other in a little village with only 9 houses in it, including the grocery store/filling station.

They both went to the nearby Westland school, about the same size as Roll, the real team that once won the Indiana State Basketball Championship and became the model for the famous movie *Hoosiers*. If you've seen that movie, you get a feeling for my upbringing, although when my parents married they moved to Greenfield, close to the Eli Lilly Plant where my father worked.

There he instrumentalized the production of Penicillin, the first antibiotic, from chicken eggs. Interesting isn't it that his father died in Europe during World War I not from battle but Influenza? My mother was a pianist, organist, and teacher. As a child, I went to sleep at night listening to her play classical piano music.

My parents believed that the best way to raise me and my two younger sisters, Margie and Suzie, was in open country near the Lilly complex. In his spare time, my father raised a few animals, including pigs, chickens, and cows you will meet later.

The field behind our house was rented to farmers, who became my first employers at the age of about 10, learning to shovel corn and later drive a tractor.

We also had a woods and spring-time ponds with fairy shrimp *who* (where I come *from* animals are persons) emerge every spring. I also loved as a kid to sneak out while the moon was full in the late spring and run naked across the soft-tilled fields in the moonlight, believing I could soak up the moon's magic rays. You can tell me by the end of the book if you think it worked.

As you read Part 1 concerning animals, you may conclude that I belong in the Pleistocene Era when humans and animals felt direct kinship with each other. If you wonder why goldfish were on my list of animals, it may be debatable whether goldfish have longer attention span than humans, but one of my aunts once said that her goldfish paid more attention to her than her husband did.

My only great teacher in high school was my math teacher, Oral Hildebrand. He had been a New York Yankees pitcher who "threw away his arm" just one batter short of getting credit for the closing win for the New York Yankees in the 1939 World Series.

He had to retire not much later to become to me a great teacher in our small high school. Like my father and my elders, he taught with *Pragmatic* methods. His version experientially was working out for myself the basic theorems of geometry.

My father's mother, widowed for 60 years until she remarried late in life, dying at 98, taught me that "proof is in the pudding, not the recipe, supposing you have one". (*Dynamic Complex Systems* friends like that way of putting things.) I am trying to entice you concerning this book. Is it working? Sorry if its not. I tried.

Academic credentials include an interdisciplinary Ph. D. from Northwestern University, learning from several distinguished professors. My fellowship allowed me to take courses and graduate seminars in any department, and I made full use of this. My Ph.D. and subsequent post-graduate training at the Gestalt Institute of Cleveland created my credentials as college professor and psychotherapist.

Despite possible "jack of all trades and master of none" accusations, I am occasionally complimented as a dependable source in relating diverse fields to each other.

For several years now, I have organized or co-organized interdisciplinary symposiums and presented papers at the annual meetings of the American Association for the Advancement of Science, Pacific Division. My publications include a scholarly monograph, three books, chapters in other books, and many articles in academic journals. My psychotherapy practice and teaching experience has included private practice in downtown La Jolla CA, the Scripps Hospital complex there, and teaching as an adjunct prof at San Diego State University.

Now you know me well enough for me to describe this as an *Em0tional Book about Emotions that Motivate Us, written for you*.

PART 1

WHAT COMES TO US *MEET JOE BLACK*

Meet Joe Black begins when a young man (played by Brad Pitt) meets a young woman (Carly Farina) in a coffee shop close to where she works as a fledgling physician at a nearby hospital. He is on his way to his new job. It looks like a romance in the making. Neither has yet learned the other's name, but we assume that they will meet again at the coffee shop. When she asks him what to do next, he says simply, *"It will come to us."*

They depart the coffee shop in opposite directions. Unfortunately, as he is walking across the street in his romantic daze, he is struck and tossed in the air first by a van and then from the opposite direction by a car, obviously killed.

Meanwhile we meet Bill Parrish (Anthony Hopkins). Parrish is the wealthy and highly respected owner of a large publishing business nearing his 65th birthday. He has been having chest pains recently but apparently not seen a physician about that yet. He has also been hearing a strange voice out of nowhere giving him an answer "Yes" to a question he has not consciously asked. But he hasn't been to see anybody like me about that either.

In his luxurious penthouse atop a tall building that night, he is having dinner with his older daughter and her husband, and with Susan, his younger daughter, who we now realize is the young woman from the coffee shop, and her boyfriend, Drew, who works for Parrish in his publishing business. She is not deeply in love with Drew, but her father has told her he hopes someday "the lightning will strike", as it did with him and her deceased mother, and she too will feel like "dancing like a dervish".

The table conversation is interrupted by a maid, who announces that Mr. Parrish has a guest at the front door. Bewildered, he tells her he will meet him in the study.

His guest appears to be the young man from the coffee shop, but we now learn instead is Death, who has "borrowed" the young man's body in order to escort Bill away soon to the other world. We now learn that the "Yes" that Bill has been hearing is the answer to the question he has not yet consciously asked, "Am I going to die?"

However, before taking Bill away, Death wants first to enter the world as a *real* person for a while, not in his usual role as a *Disembodied* visitor but as a human who can actually Experience the enthused and dramatic life that Bill illustrates, but which Death has never experienced first-hand. Bill is to be his guide in order for him to have such experiences.

He tells Bill that he will begin by having dinner with him and his family and tomorrow accompany him on his daily routines. Bewildered but agreeable since he realizes he has no real option, Bill takes Death back to the dinner table. As he is introducing him to his family, he stumbles for a name but finally comes up with Joe Black, a business associate who will be staying with him for a while.

Susan is startled but obviously disappointed that Joe's detached and awkward ways do not resemble the young man she met earlier that day. In fact, *Joe is just learning the basics of life as a human*. Like a child, he sniffs all his food before eating it, and is very awkward at first in conversation but obviously enjoys being treated as a human, just as a child would.

After Bill has departed to go to sleep, Joe wanders around the penthouse and into the pantry to discover the butler with a jar of peanut butter in his hand. The butler notices his curiosity and provides him a spoonful of it, and then another. Joe now loves peanut butter, as do most children and even adults like me, all the way though the movie. He takes a spoonful of it upside down in his mouth as a child would, and continues his walk.

The penthouse is very elaborate and has its own pool, where he meets again with Susan as she ends her swim. He tells her awkwardly, after finally taking the peanut putter spoon on her request out of his mouth, that he would like to be her friend. Still disappointed at his difference from the earlier young man, she says she has lots of friends already and needs no new ones. When Joe says he has no friends, she angrily replies that she can see why. Result: She hurts his childlike feelings.

As the movie unfolds, Joe sometimes resembles a petulant child when not getting what he wants, occasionally threatening to take Bill away sooner rather than later when Bill resists his wishes. The next day he insists impetuously on visiting Bill's supposedly private board meeting, where Drew is beginning to push for a lucrative takeover by another company. Drew resents Joe's presence, especially when Bill bluntly turns down the offer, in which Drew obviously has vested interest.

Despite Joe's thanking the board for the luscious cookies when they leave the board meeting, this is the beginning of Drew's new claim to the board privately that Bill has become demented and is no longer able to govern the board properly. What other explanation can explain the presence of this unknown "guy who loves cookies", whom Bill now takes with him everywhere and must be influencing his decision about the offer?

Meanwhile, Joe without invitation attempts one day to visit Susan on her rounds at the hospital and coincidentally meets one of her patients, an old woman "from the islands" in unbearable pain, who realizes immediately who Joe really is. Privately with her for a few moments, he resists her plea to take her away now, saying it is not yet her time, but he does *Empathize* enough to relieve her pain somewhat before leaving, afterward telling Susan he now acknowledges his presence is inappropriate.

Thus his emotional development continues as he slowly fumbles his way from *Empathy* toward *Compassion*. At first he resembles the way one of my aunts often described as her husband's better days, "hell warmed over", but as Joe becomes more comfortable with his emotions, he "grows up".

In a much later scene, he visits again the now dying old woman, who gives him some wise counsel. He listens, and for the first time, the movie seems to be telling us, he experiences not just Empathy (feeling her pain) but Compassion (reaching out and doing something about it).

He not only relieves her pain but seems to *bless* her on her way to the other world, something we assume Death had never done before. We will return to the old woman's advice later.

While Bill's power over his board is unraveling, Joe, like the young man in the coffee shop, influenced perhaps by his own developing feelings and the physical body he has borrowed, falls in love with Susan, who likes what she now sees in him. They become involved. If you have not seen the movie, I provide no spoiler here. OK?

This time *he* asks the same question *she* had asked the young man earlier. This time *she* says, "It will come to us."

At Bill's country estate where his lavish 65[the] birthday celebration is to take place, Joe at first announces to Bill that he loves Susan and plans to take her away with him to the other world. Bill is enraged that he would deprive Susan of a *real* life, and chides him that she does not even realize who he really is.

Like most first time lovers, Joe says bluntly that she loves him, as if that is enough. However, he begins perhaps to realize what he does have to tell her sooner or later. Joe rejects Bill's effort to make him change his plan, but he hesitates at the door before leaving the room.

Joe is perhaps beginning to "grow up" emotionally concerning pain and loss, which occur repeatedly in the movie, first with the old woman and now Bill. Death is getting more than he bargained for as a real human. As for most of us, however, it is the tough spots that teach us most about life.

Eventually Joe even has feelings for the young man whose body he has taken. First he not only relents in his intention to take Susan with him but compassionately rescues Bill from the takeover effort before Bill's lavish birthday party begins at his country estate.

Bill has ordered Quince, his older daughter's husband, to bring Drew to see him before his lavish birthday party begins, and Quince "delivers the package", leading Drew to believe Bill is accepting the board's decision to oust him. Bill instead is trying to trick Drew into acknowledging his plot while the board is listening on Bill's phone.

However, at a critical moment, Joe startles both Bill and Drew by announcing that it is time for the secrecy about his identity to be revealed. Bill fears what he will say, and tries to stop him, but Joe pro- cedes, stating that he is in fact an agent of the IRS.

Joe reports that he has secretly been accumulating evidence of the illegality of the takeover, and unless Drew admits his guilt and resigns from the board, he will receive "a punishment far more severe than he can possibly imagine". (After all, can *you* imagine what it would be like if the IRS ever comes after you? This would be much worse.) When Drew admits his guilt, not realizing that the board is listening by phone, Joe compassionately pats him on the back as he leaves. Bill's company is saved.

Joe later says a goodbye of sorts to Susan, asking her first if she knows who he is. As she stares into his eyes, she stutters and finally answers simply, "You are Joe". Sensitive young woman don't you think? She seems to be getting a glimpse of who he really is. However, he promises her that she will never lose what she experienced in the coffee shop, breaks from their embrace, and walks away.

Near the end of his glorious birthday party, Bill makes a moving speech to the large crowd of admirers who have gathered for the party, while Joe *with a tear in his eye* waits on a nearby hillside to take Bill away to the other world.

An attendant approaches, but when Joe asks, says he has no peanut butter. Poor Joe, life has again provided more than he expected when he started his earthly venture.

So he waits, perhaps recalling the old woman's counsel, that he return to the world where he properly belongs with "nice pictures" of his experiences to console him. Bill eventually arrives and side by side he and Bill disappear over the nearby hill as Susan watches them leave.

To her surprise, however, what appears to be Joe but is now somehow the young man from the coffee shop approaches from the other side of the hill. When Susan asks the bewildered young man what they will do next, guess what now the original young man says? "*It will come to us.*" They walk back down the hill together as fireworks flare in the sky above them. The end.

What would you say is the moral of this story? Perhaps Death is not as bad as first appears? Perhaps since Death has revived the young man in a genuine act of Compassion, he can go back to his old job with new feelings? Or perhaps if you agree with one reviewer, it is not the young man at all but Death who reappears, that he just cannot get too much of a good thing?

The last interpretation is rather cynical, unless you think he gave his old job to the young man, but surely that is not the job the young man was headed for when he was killed at the beginning of the movie. That would be even more cynical, right?

On the positive side, there does appear to be some hope for Death itself. Death is certainly a better person at the end than at the beginning, right? Personally, I'm rather proud of Death for his emotional accomplishments by the end of the movie.

However, lest you worry that there really is such a creature as Joe: Joe is no more real than hobbits and fairies in fantasies of C. S. Lewis (not to be confused with C. S. Peirce). *Meet Joe Black*, like the stories of Lewis, are for our emotional benefit. So please don't start having nightmares about Joe. He just got a little carried away with his job. Know anyone like that?

Before leaving *Joe Black*, however, a few words about the meaning of *"what comes to us"*. *Where does it come from, and what does all his have to do with animals?*

We have started with everyday human problems. Now we will turn to how animals provide a good grounding for either Joe or us as *we* grow up.

The seven Scenes of Part 1 describe the bare roots of *"what comes to us"* in animal and human sensory development. Each Scene, as stated earlier, focuses not on a particular scene in the movie but on a particular species of *animal*, meaning for our purposes any mobile (*animated*) creature, from mobile single-celled life to humans, including insects.

If you, like me, also love plants, flowers, and trees, which receive little consideration in this book, you can check out recent articles about the therapy of "forest bathing", which I practice often.

That said, on with the show. *What comes next is not a fictitious three pigs story; it is about real pigs.*

SCENE 1 PIGS: MAKING SENSE OF THINGS

I recall this as if it happened yesterday: When *very* young I am playing in the yard on the right side of our house, looking out toward the shagbark hickory tree on this side of the road, and on this side of the tree, sheets are waving in the wind on the clothes line that runs toward the catalpa tree beside me. I turn farther to the right, looking through the chain-link fence and across the lane that leads toward the barn farther to the right. Pigs are sloshing around in the mud of their pig-wallow.

They fascinate me, so I walk over to the gate leading through the fence toward them, reach up, undo the hook that holds it in place, and walk across the lane toward the pigs. They stop sloshing, turn their heads, and look at me. I look back at them. I only have a pair of shorts on and am barefooted (butter-footed as we kids called it). They have white skin like mine. Maybe they thought I am one of them with rags on.

I *sense* that I would be welcome among them, and they seem to *sense* something similar in me. I don't look all *that* much like them, but must not look like I want to eat one of them for dinner. *They look friendly to me, so I walk into the pig-wallow and sit down with them.* Grunting as I sit down in the mud, they grunt back.

We are now friends. We feel at home with each other and are having a good time sloshing around in the mud until my mother looks out the kitchen window and sees what I am doing.

Following her version of mothering instincts, she runs screaming out of the house and drags me out of the pig-wallow, scattering the poor pigs everywhere. She takes me into the house to wash off all the mud and forbids me ever to do such a filthy thing again. Knowing me all too well, however, she does not trust me never to do it again, so she demands that my father get rid of the pigs and stick to cows and chickens.

Let Your Children Eat Dirt had obviously not been written yet, and if it had been, she would never have read it. As you may imagine, I liked the book even *before* reading it.

My experience with the pigs is the earliest and fondest memory of my early childhood. To this day, I feel deep inside me that I'm really a pig.

My wife Bonnie, now "passed on" as they say where I grew up, often described me as "Messy Jesse." Whenever I came in from my extensive gardening in the "Jungle" of our huge back yard looking like I just got out of a pig-wallow, or when she often found me on the floor of the study wallowing in books, papers, and scribbled notes, I was likely to hear that greeting from her as she enters the room, and still hear echoes of it.

That moniker also fits me for my role as a psychotherapist wallowing with my clients in their messy lives, not to mention my own, especially during my Gestalt training. It also fits my proclivity for scientific obscurities like *Dynamic Complex Systems* and the unimaginable messes of James Joyce's *Finnegans Wake*. I am thankful to those pigs for all of this.

I've already used the words *Sense* and *Sensing* several times in this book. Senses lie deep within what I call our *Embodiment*, where we all start. Before that are what C. S. Peirce calls *Things*, which always surround us, visible and invisible. *Things* originate from the depths of *Reality* and describe every thing that is here before we have labels for it. You may have noticed the word *Thing* many times already in this book. So get used to it. More about things later.

"*What comes to us*" is an invisible thing that every so often Appears *out of the blue*, without our expecting it, until *now*. But it is more than just noticing something that was not there before we notice it.

Most *things* are easy to name, like hickory or catalpa tree, but it is very difficult to find a name for *"what comes to us"*. "What comes to us" resembles "Bright Ideas", but it is more like "Inklings", feelings that *precede* ideas, although ideas may result from them, as with Joe and Susan getting into their relationship. Wherever such feelings and bright ideas come from, they come from the same kind of place, wherever it is. In any event, as with Joe and Susan . It is usually a sense of *What to Think or Do Next*.

It is not, however, what is usually called *Conscience*, which usually has to do with guilt and what *not* to do. Nor is it *Temptation* to do something *Wrong*. It is more like lovers falling in love, like Joe and Susan, or on a far more modest level like little Jimmy (my nickname as a child), who was far too young to have a Conscience but could fall into a childish kind of *Empathy* (rather than *Love*) for the pigs.

It could be something as everyday as when a new possible ingredient comes to you (or your grandma) to add to a recipe. Sometimes such things emerge quickly, but may have developed slowly. Even when they emerge suddenly they can be the results of eons of earlier evolutionary experience in both us and animals, a message from the ancients, so to speak, but always tested by *Experience*.

However, they always seem to happen *before* we stop to think *about* them. Animals almost never stop to think about things at all; it just "comes to them" as they do it, but they may have learned over the eons to act that way.

Animals *can* act suddenly, as when a predator appears and it is time to fight, crouch and hide, or run for your life. An animal who hesitates or does the wrong thing in such situations may be alive one moment and dead the next. *Evolution* has taught them that.

Emotions are often considered *pre-packaged reactions*, but even when they *appear* to be, the supposed *packages* may be results of long evolutionary experience that have become habitual and ingrained, as habits usually are.

Even "packages" may still Make Sense, because they have a history of making sense. It *Makes Sense* for a Canadian goose to fly south for a winter vacation in the fall or fly back home in the spring. When it comes time to go, geese in the flock realize that the time is right, and they go. This is the result of a longstanding and *living* habit. How long do you suppose it took pigs to learn that mud is a good sun blocker?

Daniel Kahneman's distinction between *fast* (emotional) and *slow* (rational) thinking *can* be important, but can easily be exaggerated. In right and left hemisphere brain processes, the former may *appear* quickly and the latter slowly, but *Emerging Emotion* may also be slow in learning from experience, even if the final results appear suddenly. Ever notice that when Feelings just seem to appear out of nowhere?

Meet Joe Black tells us what "comes to us" emotionally may emerge slowly and unconsciously, wherever it comes *from*. So forget about simple situations when a predator is lurking. Consider the very slow stuff, like when Canadian geese "realize" it is time to fly south. It is certainly not the result of thinking reflectively. Nor is the slow stuff in your own life, like when you get fed up with your job or whatever. It just *Feels* like it is time to *Do Something* and you *Do* it. Ever had that kind of experience?

Neither the pigs nor I sat down to think about it before we got together in the pig-wallow, and neither does an athlete when doing something during a game, nor do Joe and Susan in *Meet Joe Black*. It is mainly a matter of learning from *experience* by *feeling* one's way along. *That's Life for either animals or humans. Experience is an acknowledged teacher, slow or fast.*

Things simply *emerge*, as in Joe's case when he moves from one level to another. He spontaneously loves peanut butter, but it slowly comes to Joe as he starts to open that door that perhaps the time will come for him to do what Bill is urging him to do about Susan. He is *feeling* his way along.

Arguing usually accomplishes nothing anyway. Humans persuaded against their will are un-persuaded still, right? Anybody ever try to persuade you to do something you don't *feel* fits the problems *you* face?

Thinking *about* things can sharpen sensitivity, as a telescope does, for example. Kahneman is an expert at doing this kind of thing, and his work stands for itself, but he seems to run out of gas as he comes toward the end of his book and the subject of "well being".

It may well be statistically obvious that "well being" (translation: *happiness*) is not increased for people who make more than $75-80,000 a year, but how much does that tell us? Something, but not all that much.

Joe starts as Disembodied and Detached, doing a "package" job of taking humans to the other world. He resembles Lieutenant Waters in the third movie, *Tears of the Sun*. Lt. Waters, like Joe, is just doing a "package" job in rescuing a jungle hospital physician and her associates from jungle to aircraft carrier. Very packaged job, right?

Relationships, not only between Bill and his deceased wife, Joe and Susan, or the young man in the coffee shop and Susan, are deep issues of *Making Sense* of things, and of *well-being. Nobody can tell you how to do this or even what it is, but you know when you are there when it comes to well-being. It Feels like it.*

Consider Joe. He is definitely getting more than he bargained for in his desire to experience *real* life. Joe has clearly made a lot of emotional progress since he got here. Consider yourself. Ever have complicated situations to face? Tough times, aren't they? Despite the tears, was all this worth it, to Joe or you? It is up to Joe or you to consider whether or not this make for a sense of *well-being*, right?

Put more simply, you may have had animal experiences like mine with the "pigs" in your life. You have at some time *Empathized* in a somewhat similar fashion with a cat, canary, goldfish or whatever. It all starts with your neurological and emotional roots.

It starts perhaps with a "vibration" that bonds you with an animal in the same way the I bonded with the pigs. I *feel* already that we are friends before getting in with them. At the time I have hardly any vocabulary. I just *Sense* it. It is called *Empathy*.

For now the point is that *Emotion* (*Motivation*) begins with spontaneous and complex *Senses* that grow and develop in whatever direction as we *Evolve* into the humans we become. Pigs do not have as many neurons as we do in their nervous systems, but we start where they start. We are *kindred spirits*.

The physical organs of pigs are arranged in similar locations within their bodies as in ours and their neurological systems are quite complex and constructed like ours, although if you press me, I will admit to you that I know I'm not really a pig. Their empathy for me and me for them was on a very "primal" level.

Pigs are able, however, to run complex mazes and remember things from the past that might surprise you, like *why* they are in the mud that day. Don't take them for stupid. They can amaze you. They are "aware", as I said earlier, that mud is a great sun-blocker. It is a great *Survival Strategy* that required lots of time and learning experiences to become *Habits*.

If they had fingers and toes like ours instead of double hoofs as their appendages, with an eon or two of evolution, they could be Running competition with us. I have on the wall beside my desk a photo portrait of a pig wearing glasses. Maybe someday?

Below it is a cartoon that shows a luxurious room where a pig wearing a plush jacket with a wine glass in one hand is speaking with a very plain pig, telling his visitor that it all started one day when he went to the market. (I may need to explain this if you are under 50. An old- time children's story to help us count on our fingers: This little pig went to *market*, this little pig stayed home, etc. The 5th pig cried all the way home. The *market* in the cartoon is the New York *stock market*, OK?)

So if you are *under* 50, you are now a momentary older person. If you are *over* 50, you are perhaps like me reciting it while counting on your fingers. Pigs of course don't have that any fingers.

However, you now know a little about pigs. We will come back to them in this Scene in Part 2. You could say that we and pigs live in a very large pig-wallow, right?

The next Scene concerns an *Evolutionary Process* that begins even before you are born, i.e., "hatch", whether you are a pig, chicken, or human. It begins for you and for chickens at the moment when gestation occurs and your "egg" begins to develop in order to fit well enough to develop *Survival Strategies*.

Whatever and Wherever we are then, we are prepared even before we "hatch" for what comes next. Ready for that?

SCENE 2 CHICKENS AND THEIR EGGS: GETTING OFF TO A GOODSTART

As mentioned earlier, my father worked for Eli Lilly and instrumentalized the production of Penicillin from chicken eggs. That provided me a double exposure to chickens, because not only did he take me to work with him occasionally to witness early Penicillin production, we also had chickens at home in our chicken house.

One of my first jobs was feeding the chickens. I loved the hens but hated the roosters, because I had to carry a stick for protection any time I intruded into *their* territory. I also didn't like what they did to the hens, although that was nothing compared to what Danny Hutchinson's bull did to our poor cow when my father decided when I was about 10 years old to give me an early lesson about the "birds and bees". That must have set my puberty back for months.

Several times we saved some eggs to hatch for little chicks. The baby hens we kept for the eggs they would lay someday. The roosters we kept only till they were big enough to eat, which I thought the only real reason for roosters.

I hope men are worth more than roosters, but I am not sure when I look at how many men abandon their children today. Like the roosters, all they seem to think about is sex and fighting for their territory. Sound familiar?

My father was usually a good teacher and made me learn many things for myself. When he gave me my first microscope he simply told me to go get a bottle of pond water and look to see what was interesting. It was my first adventure with protozoa, to which we will return a little later.

After learning to feed the chickens, my next job was gathering eggs. Dad simply gave me the egg basket and told me to gather the eggs. I came back wounded, saying that the hens pecked me every time I tried to reach under them for the eggs. He explained that they were just good mothers trying to protect their children, and took me out *behind* the chicken house with the basket.

He asked me what that long slender horizontal door was *for*. A light bulb came on inside my head. I raised the door and sure enough, it opened on the back on each hen's nest. Each nest was built so that the hen could not turn around safely for fear of damaging her eggs, but I could reach under her and get eggs without fear of being pecked.

Before we hatched baby chicks the first time, he helped me build a simple incubator. I learned to "bide my time" patiently for 30 days for the eggs to hatch. When it finally happened, it dumbfounded me and still does (1) imagining the incredible changes taking place in an egg before the little yellow chicks broke through the egg shell, and (2) wondering how they could immediately start walking around pecking and inspecting the world for food without a mom to tell them what to do.

C. S. (for Charles Stanley) Peirce (pronounced "purse" if you recall) introduced the world to *Pragmatism*. Most know pragmatism means "practical", but it is far more than that. His friend William James is also known as a pragmatist because of his contributions to psychology.

Embodied Cognitive Science today both appreciates James and criticize him for the same reason Peirce did over a century ago. But they haven't noticed that, because Peirce is known mainly as a natural scientist/philosopher rather than a psychologist.

James originated the famous term Stream of Consciousness. Peirce tried but failed to convince James that the primary characteristic of consciousness is not a matter of *flow* of energy in his *"stream* of consciousness", but *connectivity* within and between things.

Peirce insisted that consciousness did not resemble a *stream* so much as a *train* of connections. The primary themes of the early 20th century generally and not just in psychology were on the force of flowing "streams". Peirce had a very different orientation.

You may already have noticed that I use the word *thing* often. It was an unconscious influence of Peirce on me before I noticed how often I use it. His notion of *things* fits physics, biology, linguistics, logic, in fact almost everything about nature and humans, both individually and collectively.

For Peirce everything new emerges from other things, whatever they are. The secret is not in a dominating force flowing through things but in their own interconnected "trains".

Every thing is surrounded by *Chance* as Peirce called it over a century ago. *Chaos* is what many call it today. *Genesis* long ago called it "without form and void."

For Peirce this formless void by whatever name is constantly producing things, some producing *new* things. *Such things not only began 13.8 billion years ago, they are still happening all the time and everywhere, including within us.* Things are forever interconnecting with other interconnected things. Peirce called this the *Evolutionary Process.*

Everything from physics and biology to linguistics and logic is an Evolutionary Process. Everything emerges from interconnections, which is to say Inter-Relations between and among things. By their very nature they sometimes lead to *new and different kinds of things,* like you and me for example. We are both strange, right? There is nobody like us anywhere.

Peirce also invented Semiology, the Evolutionary study of language as *Signs*. Semiology and Logic are what they are today because of him. As things become significant and identifiable they become

Signs such as words, phrases, sentences, paragraphs, ideas, theories, symbols, paintings, music, and other forms of art.

Thanks largely to him, Logic is no longer the rather mechanical discipline it once was and in some places still is. For him logic, too, is Evolutionary, always evolving..

Consider the Evolution of Neurological systems in both chickens and us that begins before our birth. Chemistry is important too, as in genes and hormones, but the gist of our neurological system is its billions upon billions of neurons interacting with each other. Those interactions eventually create consciousness, and also language, one of our primary methods to interconnect with each other. Peirce's version is different from Darwin's, as you can see.

Interconnections for him make things *Active* and possibly *Creative*. In Scenes ahead this will be described in terms of today's *Complex Systems*. The neurosystems of little chicks and little children are Dynamic Complex Systems at work.

So let's talk about chickens and us *before* we broke through our egg sacs and fell into the outside world of external interconnected things. The focus is on the *Neurosystem* already emerging inside an egg.

Here it is not a matter of the proverbial "egg *and* I." Here the egg *is* I, but *I* at first begins inside a shell, although entering the outside world is dramatically different. It reminds me of a poem by my poet friend Arthur Raybold who wrote of his dog trying to lick the rain falling on the *outside* of a window when he was on the *inside*. It is the same rain either way for chick, dog, or you, but now you are outside and *in* it. Inside is simply preparing you *for* it.

Moving outside for any of us may be difficult. (Ask your mom, she knows.) The eggshell is fairly easy to break for both chicks and us compared to most "windows". When any of us are born we are just waiting to break through that window.

Small wonder that we cry. We can't wait to get out of there.

Peirce had no access to neurological research comparable to ours today, so some of his work may now seem dated, but his *train* was obviously on the right track a century before time finally caught up to him. Had he understood the sheer complexity of a "train" of the billions upon billions of neurons in our human neurological system, he would be very pleased with *Embodied Cognitive Science*.

This Scene focuses on the processes taking place in the fertilization of either the chicken egg or you. So think of yourself before you "hatched" in the delivery room.

In fact of course we are forever hatching. We don't stop when we are born. This book ends in a delivery room. *It basically means you potentially hatch every day you wake up.* By the time you are born, supposing you escape possible handicaps, you are well equipped for what faces you, including every single day you wake up and every conversation you ever have with anyone, including the one you are having now with me.

"Great day in the morning" as my grandma often said to me. We will come back to *days* occasionally as we proceed toward the end of the book.

The dynamics taking place inside an egg are very complex and defy precise description. The best general model to me is that of C. H. Waddington, a geneticist who declared that describing an incubating egg in two dimensional models is inadequate to describe its complexity. Instead Waddington suggested a *Three Dimension Epigenetic Landscape* resembling a path of paths down through a complex valley of valleys.

However, it's not a river flowing, but genetic ball rolling. bouncing, and interacting with things on its way toward the "shore" where the egg hatches into a little whatever, whether a chicken or you when your mommy "hatched" you.

Embodiment

You were then incredibly gifted and experienced in dealing with the problems of your ancestors even before you were born. For further information you can buy Waddingon's book listed in Recommended Books, or you can also go online to Waddington's Epigenetic Landscapes for illustrations.

Although Waddington confesses that his models, like those of Dynamic Complex Systems theorists, are incapable of including all the details, they are better than two dimensional graphs, and provide graphic illustrations of what is happening not only in a baby chick's egg but yours inside your mommy's tummy during the nine months of your gestation in nine months as compared to a chick's 30 days.

Is it any wonder that traditional scientists often throw up their hands and cry: "What is the use of all this complexity? We need to simplify it." Dynamic Complex Systems, however, are not always easy to simplify. As you know, weather forecasts are often wrong, except in very wide probabilities. In Dynamic Complex Systems, you have to be careful what you ignore.

My sub-atomics Physicist friend Jay Raghavan can tell you about this or if you can handle it, the book for such things he recommends is Murray Gel-Mann's *The Quark and the Jaguar*. Both authors are found in Recommended Books. They dive even deeper than neurons for our origins.

As Peirce says, there are times when you have to allow *Results* to speak for themselves when basic Causes may not be even be knowable.

Esther Thelen and Linda Smith have demonstrated clearly, for ex- ample, that how a child learns to walk is a lesson in "simple" dynamics that doesn't fit traditional models of learning at all. Not much space here to describe this, but imagine you are watching a robot and a small child like you were once "learning" to walk.

For you it was easy. For a robot it is incredibly difficult even with elaborate programming.

First you learn to crawl when your parents held you horizontally a little off the ground. Your feet and arms start waving, they put you on the ground, and you take off crawling. I once watched a young child learning this in the aisle between rows of seats in a plane. It was hilarious watching the parents try to catch her suddenly racing up the aisle. I said, "She'll be walking sooner than you think."

After *you* accomplished that feat, they held *you* upright by *your* little hands, set *your* little feet on the ground, "walked" *you* around a while till *you* got the *feel* of it, and gradually let go so *you* could do it without their help, and the parade was on, laughing all the way for your new accomplishment. In my case when I eventually made it all the way to the pig-wallow.

Robots can only do this with very intricate programming. Only recently have robots been able to keep walking when pushed or shoved a little without falling on the floor. A child learns quickly from *Experience*, but a robot does not learn directly from *Experience*.

A child is *Alive*. A robot is *not*. How is that for a start? Perhaps robots will be alive someday, but don't hold your breath. Researchers have for several years now been attempting to create computers that can learn like humans do. The vast promises of AI, Artificial Intelligence, have been vastly overestimated,

If you are into this, I advise reading Melanie Mitchell's book on that subject listed in Recommended Books at the end of this one. She writes beautifully concerning her personal experiences (in a more academic and sophisticated way than me) concerning AI programs and predictions, which have actually made hardly any progress at all. In brief, they still have a very long way to go.

A robot is born in a very different kind of maternity ward, has a very different kind of body, and thinks and behaves in a very different way. The only thing you can say now is to a robot is: "Get a life."

Computers are wonderful *tools* but not at least for a very long time, if ever, will they be our *replacements*. We have had many more years of learning from Experience than they have.

We will come to *Tools* much later in the book. However, the focus in his chapter is that we shouldn't underestimate the *on-board* equipment we have at birth.

We have 13.8 billion years of nature's Experience on our side, if we don't blow it. Chickens have not changed nearly as much as we have during that time, but we both have amazing Bodies and learn from there till now from Experience.

SCENE 3
CANADIAN GEESE: WHERE TO GO NEXT

Scene 2 is about basic neurological development *before* little chicks or you hatch. Even inside the shell, everything is already directed toward the future. *In Scene 3, the chick and you are still going somewhere different,* but *now it can be somewhere else than where you were in the egg. You are now in the outside world.*

Inside the egg you had little to say about anything. You just do where you are told, so to speak. Now you gradually learn to have a say in things, including "Where are you going, and how will you get there?" It is still about *Intentionality*, "consciousness (of)" as early phenomenologists put it.

However, now you live on the edge of the future and what happens next in the world of "out there somewhere". As you grow up, you are more and more on your own, whether pig, chicken, Canadian goose, or human.

As a human, your egg now has hands and feet, and five senses to help you along, and the senses are far more sensitive than impressions made on a blank slate. They are *Active and Alive.*

We become what in Complex Systems are called *Self-organizing Agents*, always *going* somewhere and *doing* something to get there, whether physically or psychologically.

Whether animal or human, you know where you are by constantly *reshaping* your *Gestalts (configurations)* of how to get elsewhere as part of an ever-changing Experience in the outside world today is always different from yesterday. *If days are always the same symbolically or actually, you are dead.*

So you are forever changing not just your space but your sense of Orientation. *You as well as Canadian Geese now live in a far bigger chicken yard that little chicks ever dream of as they grow up, and it requires Common Sense to go wherever is next. Such senses may be different for pigs, chickens, or even geese than humans, but in any case, common sense is an Active rather than a Passive phenomenon.*

That is what Making Sense is for. Trying to step outside your Senses to think about things as a human can bring both advantages and disadvantages. Sometimes a map helps, for example, but sometimes you don't need one because you can find your way on your own with your *Senses. That is what they are there for.* Do that and pigs, chickens, and geese will be proud of you.

I had received my Ph. D and was teaching at a new state college in Michigan and living in nearby Midland, located as the name suggests in the center of the state. I describe my work there elsewhere.

Mark, Sheila, and Biker Mike, a Viet Nam veteran, were students in my Environmental Learning classes. They told me of *Shiawassee Flats*, a major feeding station for Canadian Geese and other migrating birds like ducks and swans as they flew south in the fall for their winter vacations and back home to Canada in the spring.

As locals, they knew routes through the woods and out onto the levies, where grain was regularly dumped for the bird *food stop*. For several years I now I do that at the Bushfire Kitchen, Temecula for a meal six days a week, but geese only stop at the Flats twice a year. And where the Bushfire Kitchen is 15 minutes from home, their stops at the Flats require days of flying to get there and more days to get where they are going, but in both cases, our "flight" is *Intentional*.

Walking directly out and onto the levies into the midst of thousands of circling birds was like walking into a National Geographic Special. Today a limited access road has been constructed through the flats, and it is closed during migration seasons, so it is reportedly no longer possible to make that trek today. For me and my students and my family it became an Awesome experience often during my 10 years in Michigan before my own migration to California.

Canadian Geese are known for their V-shaped flying formations. They are wise enough to learn from Experience how such flight formations make it possible to utilize winds and updrafts in order to minimize energy required for hundreds of air miles back and forth playing follow the leader.

Geese are very intelligent creatures. You may assume "the leader" lets the others know where to go, but that's a bit off the mark. There are many leaders. In order for each leader to economize its energy, when it tires it drops back and, another is ready to take over. So it is not a single leader who knows the way to where they are going, and they never miss even by a few miles either the Flats or their eventual destinations.

It is not geese alone who have such memories. Where I live now on the edge of Murrieta, California, I'm often visited by a great Blue Heron, who likes the climate here all year long and has no need to migrate long distances. Years ago it started "migrating" to the half-acre back yard I call our *Jungle*, the back of which has a view of Mt. Palomar in one direction, the San Jacinto Mountains in another.

It has been looking for fish for dinner, and its excellent memory tells it every year since that first trip that I had created a small fish pond. The first year I bought some goldfish, some of whom I hoped would grow much bigger.

However, I went out one day to see this long legged blue heron, as tall as I am, eating every one of them from the pond. Not only that, it still comes looking every year to my fish pond, although frustrated Jesse stopped stocking it with fish a few years ago. That is what I call good memory. But I would now miss the heron if it stops coming, so I'll stock it again next year but now call it my Heron Pond.

The memory of Canadian geese is similar but happens on a collective level, and they, like the heron, don't need road maps to know where they are going. Instead of road maps they have what could be called *especially good sense. This year* a family of Gold-Capped Orioles decided they like me so much they are staying in my Jungle all summer instead of just passing through here on their way North in the Spring.

Geese never stop to think, however, about where they are going. They have no maps or travel books. It just "comes to them" from having such good sense and memory that away they go. *They learn Spontaneously Through Experience*, as we do most of the time.

So the issue is not whether Experience needs Rationality for a base but whether rationality needs Experience for a base. Unless rationality is Embodied, which is to say Embedded, Rationality has little practical use.

I'll approach this subject several times as we fly our own course in this book. We'll go into more depth in Scene 3 of Part 2, but *Experience always means moving into the future*. According to early 20[the] century phenomenologists, it is the primary characteristic of human and animal consciousness.

Life's evolutionary processes, including Intentionality, begin long before the appearance of the human mind and eventually conscious reflection. It originates in Peirce's insights into Primal *Inter-Connectivity*.

Nature, like us, makes mistakes but learns from them, just as we do, and it does this without thinking about it reflectively at all. Have you ever made a mistake? Of course you have. The question is when you learned from it and how many mistakes it takes for the learning. Experience does that all the time.

Experience teaches you both emotionally and even reflectively. Rationality learns this not from Socrates but from Experience. Without Experience, Rationality is Disembodied. Disembodied Rationality might easily justify Genocide as an important way to control over-population. Ask Adolf Hitler.

Thanks mostly to Peirce, as stated earlier, logic shifted its practices in the last century, and Logic today is a much more dynamic and evolutionary in its methods. Evolution may always be unfinished in one way or another, but always learns from Experience.

As Roseanne Roseannadanna of TV fame says, "There is always something." Peirce would like that. *The end of things is always Open, as Life itself is.* You and Canadian geese may make a mistake and land on a snapping turtle who scares you off. However, "Practice makes Perfect", as my elders often said, although none of us of course is perfect, so it is always an unfinished job, right?.

But Evolution is always aimed toward perfection. *The Test is What Lasts Over Time.* Contrary to what recent "rationalists" insinuate, *Empathy makes important sense, or it wouldn't be here for eons.*

Admittedly, Empathy is a Primal Experience, not a more complex one like Compassion. Joe Black and the rest of us only gradually move from Empathy to Compassion. Even "death warmed over" with some experience can learn without thinking about it.

What "comes to you" is a cat of many colors. It "came to Einstein" that space and time do not proceed in a "straight line", they bend; in short, the result is his Theory of Relativity, which solves problems never solved before. There are many shades and grades of Experience that "come to us" in science as well as every day experience. *Experience is not stupid. It is definitely smarter than Disembodied Reason.*

What "comes to us" to do next is similar to what comes to a flock of Canadian geese in how to get to Shiawassee Flats. Life is full of what "comes to us". It "comes to you" that you need Sam or Sally in order to help you get where you want to go in life.

It is dangerous to separate emotion and reason, except for certain kinds of projects. Emotion (Motivation) and Experience are always there to help you, like the Canadian Geese, to get to where you want to go. Does that make sense?

"We learn by going how to get where we want to go." That fits the life of geese as well as ours. In the process of "what comes to us" we learn as we *feel* our way along. *Life's line can be bent, of course, but then Life seldom runs in straight lines.*

Changes can be radical, like when I was young and our home is struck by a tornado. The sky turns black in the middle of the afternoon, it begins to rain, and the wind is blowing very hard. Everything looks bad.

We huddle together in the corner of the living room farthest away from the windows. We hear very loud rumbling and then the tornado suddenly hits. BANG! And almost as suddenly it is gone.

Fortunately we are not directly in its path and our brick house is relatively untouched. However, tornadoes are strange. I recall that it sucks a sheer curtain through a crack in one living room window so tightly that the window has to be broken to get the curtain free.

But the sun is now shining outside and peace and quiet appear as suddenly as the tornado had. My dad says it is ok to go outside. There is a double rainbow shining in the east, and the grass is now bright green, although the deep-rooted cedar tree outside the front porch now sits at a 45 degree angle.

I walk around the house and look toward the barn, then run back to the living room to say that our barn had "got gone", completely gone. It was like a scene near the end of *Twister*. They lose their barn too, and their house too was relatively undamaged. But we find pieces of our barn miles away.

Fortunately we had stopped having cows by then, and the chicken house was still there, untouched. One local story was that one farmer ended up with 8 new cows that were never claimed by anybody. That story may have been a stretch, but tornados are strange.

Sometimes what "comes to us" comes with such a Bang, but other times slowly and quietly, like when you seem to sense a solution to an important problem even *before* you know it. It is the "I knew this deep inside me before I realized it" kind of thing.

I often have this kind of experience when writing and feel that I am just a stenographer taking down dictation. It just seems to keep going. My favorite expression concerning such experiences is: "I just work here." Have you ever had that experience?

I talk about this kind of experience in "The Parable of the Chicken House", an article I once wrote for the *Journal of Environmental Science and Engineering*. I list only books in Recommended Books at the end of this book, although if you write to me, I can help you find it.

What comes to us is an amazing complex of multiple sources that occur "before we stop to think about it". We act spontaneously on what is often called "Common Sense", the only way to get anywhere in most animal species.

I was driving one day to a location in the mountains I had visited years ago that has no physical address so neither a roadmap nor my GPS helped. So I *felt* my way. I recalled this or that landmark from years ago, but at one point the road just didn't "feel right", and I realized I was lost.

After retracing my steps to where "things feel right", and notice a road I had not seen because undergrowth had covered everything around the intersection since I was there earlier, so I take that road and it leads me where I want to go. Life is full of such experiences. They are parts of *feeling our way around*.

You could say that this book is meant to be a Shiawassee Flats feeding station on your way to wherever. Learn from your Common or Uncommon Sense and Experience, and you are usually likely to get there.

SCENE 4
BATS: SENSING THE SURROUNDINGS

Bats are among the most marvelous of earth's creatures. I recently installed a bat house in my Jungle that will house as many as 100 bats. I probably won't get that many, but if I do, I'll install another bat house.

Human fear of bats is overblown. Have you or anyone else you know ever been bitten by a bat? Almost no one else has either. Fear of bats is often because of fear of contracting Rabies from them. That is possible, but extremely unlikely. Less than 1 person in the United States dies each year from a bat bite. It is over 35,000 times more likely that you will die in a car wreck this year. Does that keep you from driving or riding in a car?

By far the greatest risk with bats is a *sick* bat. Bats, like most animals, are susceptible to Rabies. A bat in your house is probably seeking refuge because it is sick, so call Animal Control to solve the problem. Do the same if you find a sick bat anywhere outside. Don't try nursing it back to health.

However, if you think you have been bitten by *any* wild animal, go quickly to an emergency room. That is just Common Sense.

Bats have many creatures on their list of creatures to bite, and humans are not even on it. The main reason they might fly close to you is probably for mosquitos they find close to you.

Vampire bats are of course another matter. There are 40 species of bat in this country, and vampire bats are extremely rare here. *Virtually all bats in this country are our protectors, not our enemies.*

Mosquitos carrying diseases are really the most dangerous creatures on earth. If you want to swat something, try mosquitos. I personally consider bats my friends. I usually swim on my back, so that above day or night I can see stars, clouds, planes, satellites, drones, and of course bats. A very big owl worried me once, but when it saw I was not a duck, it flew away. When I see a bat, I just wiggle hello with my fingers.

Besides, they are cute little creatures, and built much like us. As with pigs, their organs are in the same locations as ours. *They are mammals like us, can have no more than one child a year, etc.* Their "wings" are remarkable but very different from bird wings. Bird wings resemble our shoulders and elbows. Bring your hands together in front of you. Hold your hands still and wave your elbows up and down together. That is how most birds fly.

Now hold your wrists, hands, and fingers in front of you and wave and wiggle around your wrists and fingers. Notice the flexibility you have in your wrists and fingers and how you can do different maneuvers with each hand, not necessarily synchronizing them with each other. Bats fly in almost any direction quickly and efficiently, especially since their "fingers" are webbed together for aeronautical "wings".

Besides that, bats do not have feathers, but skin and hair. However, their hairs are far more sensitive than the hair on your head or body. And their "ears" are far more sensitive than yours. Despite what you may have been taught, they hear quite well, but they also *hear* by sonar more than *see* the presence of a mosquito. Even the bat's good eyes cannot in the dark from a distance *see* small mosquitos, but who are doomed by *sonar*. They cannot hide in the dark from bats like they do from you.

Even moths, who also have sonar equipment, do not stand much a chance with a bat close at close range, although they can Sense a bat from a distance. Moths can also perform aerobatic antics, but not usually quickly enough to evade a bat. It would be like me trying to keep the basketball away from Steph Curry. The bat and Steph win. The moth and I lose.

Embodiment

My electronically equipped night-time security system allows me to watch bats dart about in my back yard. Even Steph cannot do antics like that, and besides, he can't fly. Humans also have only 180 degrees viewing field. Eagles have 260, but thanks to solar assistance, bats have a nearly wrap around 360, even in pitch darkness. And besides they have those intricate "wings".

Lets face it, humans are usually afraid of bats because they are afraid of the dark. Why do you sleep with a little light on at night? Most likely, it is not just so that you can find your way to the bathroom, right?.

As you know, when I was young I liked running naked across the spring fields in the moonlight, but *not* on a moonless night. Not only were there no magic moon rays to absorb, I might not see a big snapping turtle or snake until too late. Besides everybody knows there are goblins in pitch-black dark.

Bats are among the most sensitive and agile creatures on earth, far more so than humans. Bats are especially well adapted to pitch-black nights. They have sonar and we don't, but that is only a beginning. It is really because of *their over-all agility and sensitivity to the environment*. No wonder there are about 1,000 bat species on earth.

I was awestruck at thousands of Canadian geese and other migratory birds swirling around me at Shiawassee Flats. The closest that I have come to with bats is on my big screen TV where I see 20 million bats living in a huge cave in Texas come swirling out into the summer evening sky. Think of how many mosquitos they eat for snacks every night to the tune of nearly 100 mosquitos per bat per hour. Are you favorably impressed? I hope so.

Do they dine on anything but mosquitos? The answer is Yes, but few insects you love. To me mosquitos are even worse than roosters, OK?

So what does that have to do with us? Put it this way. Unlike bats, most of us animals have weaknesses. We, like snapping turtles, can't turn around or back up very fast and we don't have thick shells to protect us. Some snapping turtles weigh 30-40 pounds or even more in the deep swamps. There they seldom need to back up.

I did feel quite superior when reaching behind one could grab its rough tail, pick it up, and carry it back to our watering tank for a few days (when we stopped having cows), and later carry it closer to its intended destination, Danny Hutchinson's pond. So I felt like Steph Curry instead of Jesse.

Dad said snapping turtles are edible, and we could cut one up for turtle soup, but I didn't like that idea. Actually I not only respected my snapping turtle friends but loved them, as I'm sure Steph does his opponents. At least he acts like it.

The point here is that most creatures have both advantages and disadvantages. Bats have hardly any disadvantages. There are so many of them, perhaps hundreds of millions on earth. They are an estimated 20 percent of all animal species.

Bats have no real competitors. They are too quick, flexible, and versatile to lose in nightly competition with their foe, and are never at- tacked from the rear. Batman is not crazy. It would be fun to be a bat. I mean, give me a break here, OK?

We will unpack the bat subject in more detail in Part 2, but allow me before we move on to provide an illustration from the field of Complex Systems and the world of *Attractors* and *Affordances*.

When one Dynamic Complex System enters the field of another, it is similar to when bats enter into an environment that includes a swarm of mosquitos.

Some but not all *things* remain the same when one Complex System meets another. Some things in the field remain more or less the same as when bats arrive. They may continue to be what they already were, acting the same way they always do. Within the environment, however, when a bat intrudes, it becomes a *Self-Organizing Change Agent*, the swarm of mosquitos becomes a *Basin of Attraction*, and individual Mosquitos *Fixed-Point Attractors*.

So the bat changes the Basin of Attraction, but little outside it. Most things remain the same things doing the same old things, except for Jesse, who may be happy to have the bat there but does nothing about it. The tree will still be the same tree, the rock the same rock, and Jesse the same old friend of bats, although the arrival of the bats may *prevent* a bad change *for* him by protecting him from mosquito bites and a possible virus.

So a Dynamic Complex System, whether in physics, emotion, or society is no simple matter when considering changes that occur within that system, and within the field surrounding it.

So bats become *"Self-Organizing Change Agents"* as they seize their *Affordances* in diving for the mosquitos. The bats have snacks; thus the mosquitos are gone. Jesse is still there, but now as happy as he was as a kid eating roosters for dinner.

The lightning or tornado has struck and has passed, and now the place looks "more or less" like it did before this happened, except for the missing mosquitos.

In the larger environment, the magical rays of the moon continue to shine its magic rays for Jesse. Without the mosquitos, he praises the moon and thanks the bats.

If you are still terrified by bats, of course, the story becomes more a *Repeller* rather than an *Attractor*, and for the story Jesse himself becomes a *Repeller* for attempting to make bats *Attractors*. Sorry about that. Will you forgive me?

However, I don't want to leave the impression that self-organizing agents, whether animal or human. Are necessarily disruptive and destructive and predatory like a bat is in a basin of mosquitos.

Consider me entering a gathering one evening that includes a beautiful blond, Bonnie. Jesse was no bat looking for a victim, nor was Jesse a victim when Bonnie saw me. So changes can be very positive on both ends of the Attractors.

This is an attempt to make it clear here that *Attractor* interactions can result in *Life* rather than *Death*.

I once heard the scientist John Lilly say that his first words to his wife were: "Where have you been all my life?" And her answer was: "Waiting for you." So that Experience consisted of two Self-Organizing Agents interacting with each other, and the contact was very positive for both. So was my first contact with Bonnie, although Lilly's line never occurred to me until later.

Meanwhile, bats have a wonderful home life if 20 million of them can live together all summer in the same house, Bracken Cave in Texas. Not only do they remove zillions of mosquitos from becoming threats for us, they have a good home life.

Except for vampire bats, the vast majority of changes created by bats are meanwhile for *our* good, despite the fact that among many humans they are so maligned.

And, bats get along far better with each other than we do. In the 20 million bats living happily in one house, there is next to no crime rate among them, and 20 million of them fly in and out of the same garage at nearly the same time, and with their incredible awareness of everything happening around them, their traffic accident rate and traffic deaths is almost zero.

If they were us in that cave they would need a police force of at least a million bat officers, 5 hospitals, and 20 jails. I mean, give me a break here.

There may be bats in my mental belfry, but bats are always welcome *at* (but not *in*) my house, as I said earlier.

So does that make you feel better, at least about me, if not bats? I hope so. If not, I'll give up and we can go now to the next scene. You are *sure* to like Momma Bear.

SCENE 5
BEARS: TRIAL AND ERROR

In an effort to find a good environment for Bonnie's failing health, we moved "up the hill" into the San Jacinto Mountains where our home was several miles up and beyond the quaint little village of Idyllwild.

This put us 6,000 feet above sea level, clearer air, and a remote setting. It was perched with a deck looking down to Idyllwild, across the valley from sheer Lilly Rock used by rock climbers. My sick jokes at the time was watching novice rock-climbers fall down the face of Lilly Rock. Just kidding; I never saw one fall.

Everything was peaceful and relaxing, just what Bonnie (and I) needed. I drove down to my office and teach a very full 2-3 days a week. The rest of the week we had peace and tranquility. We loved it in the mountains and had great neighbors.

Then one day I see a Black Bear nosing around our Jacuzzi. I assumed the bear was female because she only weighed 130-140 pounds. Males weigh 200 or more. And she did not try to tear into the Jacuzzi, just looked curious. (From our earlier experience at Warner Hot Springs we knew Black Bears love hot springs.)

A few days later I am sitting in the Jacuzzi, watching climbers fall off Lilly Rock and notice what looks like the same bear not far away watching me. So I, perhaps foolishly, leave the Jacuzzi open and go into the house to see what she would do.

Soon after I leave, she climbs onto our deck and gets into the Jacuzzi. Over the next few weeks I leave the Jacuzzi open whenever she appears, and in time instead of going into the house, I stay in the big Jacuzzi and beckon her to come in with me.

Eventually she does, and interesting Experiences follow. Again, perhaps foolishly, I take a jack-knife with me and lay it at my side, thinking that I as a 6' 3", 200 pound fairly athletic guy with a good knife could handle a 130-140 pound bear. It came to me later that she has the equivalent of 5 knife-like claws in each paw, and I would quickly have lost a fight with her despite my weight advantage. But by then we had become friends.

I discover that she loves peanut butter as much as Joe Black and I, for me crunchy peanut butter and strawberry preserves sandwiches, which I still love today on Dave's Many Seed Organic Bread, sometimes using honey instead of preserves, recalling all the tales of Bears and Bees. More about Bees in Scene 7.

Surprise! One day she appears with her young cub. So I again use the ritual of gesturing toward the cub with a peanut butter sandwich in my hand. Joe Black would have been proud of us. It all went beautifully for several weeks.

Then on a fateful day when Bonnie's daughter Dominique is visiting us. (Bonnie and I were married for 30 years before her passing, but we each had 4 children from our first marriages.) Dominique loved watching the cub eating a sandwich.

I'm sitting foolishly and innocently as Momma Bear starts to reach toward me, probably for another sandwich. However, Bonnie's instincts tell her that my bear friend might be reaching not for a sandwich but to grab and eat me instead of the sandwich.

Or perhaps it was that Bonnie didn't like the idea of my getting all that close to another female, even a bear, putting her claws into me. I will tell a story about her capers like that later. In any event, Bonnie comes out on the top of the stairs, leading down to the Jacuzzi, screaming at the top of her voice.

Never underestimate the power of an angry woman. Have you ever seen the movie *Chicago*? Momma bear and her cub flee in terror. They never appear at our house again. However, this happens not all that long before we move down-hill to Murrieta and closer to medical care for Bonnie.

We missed Idyllwild and did buy a small "get away" place in Idyllwild itself for a few years until Bonnie was no longer to make that trip, but there were no bears in town. Here in Murrieta we live on the east side of town, and have a small building on the hill at the back of our "Jungle" we call the Fort from the deck of which we could see the mountains where Idyllwild is.

I never learned what happened to Momma Bear. Perhaps she simply feared for her baby's life, or even her own. Perhaps someone down-hill turned her and her cub over to Animal Control. Perhaps someone shot them both thinking they were doing the world a favor. Or perhaps she decided her baby was full enough of peanut butter sandwiches and it was time to migrate. I like the last interpretation best.

Some animals adjust to the presence of humans fairly easily. They have never read the book on Coping Skills by Albert Dreyfus that will be featured in the next two Scenes, but given those standards my bear friend and I cope quite well, and without either of us even getting killed.

It is surely obvious in both this scene and the next that no human invented Coping Skills, neither Albert Dreyfus nor anyone else. Coping skills go back to the earliest animals. *Animals and insects were developing and practicing coping skills long before humans appeared on earth.*

The Black Bear species in our country migrated here originally from northern Asia millions of years ago. Bears are versatile and intelligent and have survived virtually everywhere in the northern hemisphere and in South America. (Koalas are actually marsupials with pouches, so they don't count.)

This Scene illustrates only a short-list for all Coping Skill stages: Trial and Error. They are also basic to Scientific Method, but there too nature has been practicing such skills longer before those official methods emerged. Perhaps not only animals but Nature from its very beginning has practiced them.

There are lots of stories about bears, but no bear has ever written one about humans. If they did Momma Bear could have written one about weird humans like me. *In any event, not only do Bears practice Coping Skills, they are also Scientists, so in the next few paragraphs it's not obvious who is the scientist and who is the test tube.*

Consider that my bear friend, not just me, is conducting Experiments, as Life had taught her to do. You may think this a stretch, but perhaps she was sitting there several times before I noticed her watching me in the Jacuzzi. Perhaps she was just waiting for the right *Affordance* to launch *her* Experiment.

Bears, as I said, have been on earth far longer than we have. *She also knew from her Evolutionary History that patience can pay off. So who says this story is a stretch?*

Maybe she gets her chance and takes it, then repeats her experiments as good scientists do, and they work every time. She gets not only access to the Jacuzzi but peanut butter and jelly sandwiches. So she calls in her lab assistant, her cub, to savor the success of her theory. But when my department chair decides this experimenting are getting out of hand, it has gone far enough.

So who was the scientist and who was in the test tube? We both were. We were just polishing our experiments and developing more complex theories as we went. Happens in labs all the time.

Does this make sense? Of course it does. And all this not only demonstrates how trial and error work in Coping Skills but scientific method, and it also demonstrates how Complex Systems work.

Complex Systems can be very complex. How about Bonnie's sudden appearance that frightened Momma Bear and her cub away?

Once upon a time in a gathering at the Directors home following one of her jazz dance performances and before we seriously discussed the subject of marriage, Bonnie notices across the room a young woman she thinks is paying too much attention to me.

She marches directly across the room and up to her, puts her finger in the woman's face and says, "Stay away from him. He is mine." The poor woman just turned around and walked away.

Can you imagine now how complex factors can possibly be in a Science Laboratory? And also how complex Dynamic Systems can operate?

So I've not only quickly introduced Trial and Error Coping and Scientific Method but the Dynamics of Complex Systems too, including Business and Relationship Dynamics all in one little episode.

Again, what do you want, egg in your beer?

Incidentally, this account of my bear friend may sound like a three bears story, but it is as I said, this story is about real, not fictional, animals.

For a really complex bear story, read William Faulkner's story "The Bear", a classic in American literature. In Walter Rideout's William Faulkner Seminar for graduate students, I wrote a paper on I called Faulkner's "Stoicism" based on that story. He tried unsuccessfully to have it published, and my paper paled quickly into the scholarly fog long ago. This little Scene on bears may last a little while, but not nearly as long as Faulkner's "The Bear".

Meanwhile, consider how it "comes to me or to you" what to have the next meal. What comes to me to is a peanut butter and strawberry preserves sandwich, which as I think *about* it would not only satisfy that slightly gnawing feeling in my stomach but would provide a wonderful reward for finishing this chapter.

Embodment

If you don't already have a plan for your next meal, perhaps you will find yourself considering a peanut butter and jelly sandwich. Be a kid again. Joe Black, Momma Bear, and I will be proud of you.

SCENE 6
RACCOONS: COPING SKILLS

This time the story is about Raccoons, which is since we moved down-hill from the mountains to Murrieta where I still live since Bonnie's passing.

One evening several years ago I am sitting on the back patio when I see two black shining eyes in our "Jungle". I had wondered why all the cat food had been disappearing during the night. Those black shining eyes say it is a Raccoon.

This is not my first rodeo where " Ah cum frum". I headed for more cat food. Foolish Jesse begins doing what all the books say not to do, feeding with her own bowl of cat food. However, on learning not to feed raccoons cat food exclusively or they get too fat, I soon start blending it with things like fruit and nuts as the next few weeks roll by.

Raccoons are very intelligent creatures, smarter than dogs or cats. They are intensely curious and quite often mischievous, thanks to their adept paws that operate like fingers. They are known to open door- knobs to get into houses and other buildings, and then making every- thing a mess while looking for food. I gave her an egg one evening and watched her delicately turning it over and over before breaking it on a rock and eating what was inside.

This time Foolish Jesse decides *not* to get well enough acquainted to have her sit on my lap, although it would have been easy. I learned raccoons are temperamental, unpredictable, and even treacherous, and have very sharp teeth. But even worse, I might be conditioning her to be too friendly with people, leading to her fluffy tail ending up on someone's raccoon-skin hat.

So I always stay a foot or so away so we don't get all *that* friendly. Where my acquaintance with Momma Bear only lasts a few months, my acquaintance with my raccoon friend lasted several years and through several stages of Coping Skills described by Hubert Dreyfus, whose book is listed in Recommended Books.

Stage 1 is Novice. A Novice in any Coping Skill begins with a few basic rules of operation. In learning to drive a car it includes learning basics like accelerators, brakes, and rules of the road. (We will discuss more of the philosophy of Dreyfus and Martin Heidegger's influence on him in Part 2, but here we will focus simply on the basic stages of Coping Skills.)

The Novice Stage may require a long time in some coping skills, but this stage is usually short. However, basic "rules" of the game are important, whether learned from a book or from elders.

In a scene in *Hoosiers*, the classic movie in which a tiny high school wins the state championship against a huge city high school, the coach (Gene Hackman) takes his team for the first time to the enormous Butler Fieldhouse. His team in has played only in gyms with only a few rows of spectators, so they are dumbfounded.

To settle them down, the coach has his players measure the court, goal, etc. to show them that all the measurements where they will play are exactly the same as in their little gym at home, so if their attention is on the game, they play just they do at home.

To me there is no better argument for Stage 1 in any Coping Skill. You have to get used to what you are doing, and learn not to be distracted from what needs to be done.

Basic "rules" for Dreyfus are not only in driving but in playing chess. Unless you first learn the basic *moves* and *basic strategies* involving each piece on a chess board, you cannot play the game well. You can imagine parallels in a vast field of similar coping skills.

Whatever the skill, the novice does not learn through *Experience* yet, but from *getting used to things* safely, usually learning from a coach or mentor.

It is impossible to describe just what these rules are for my raccoon friend, but animals, like us, learn from their elders. One basic "rule" for my new friend was probably was that cat food is good, no matter what you have to do to get it. Mine included the rule not to feed raccoons too much cat food.

Stage 2 is Advanced Beginner. This begins with learning from early Experiences but still in a safe, non-risky kind of space. I personally learned the hard way the importance of this stage in junior high school basketball. As a slow learner with a desperate coach, I skip over this stage too quickly when playing my first basketball game against a non-practice team.

Raccoons never seem to get all that nervous, but I am a stage-hand "basket case". As a tall, skinny, and fast-growing kid, I am nervous. Every day the basket is not exactly where it was yesterday, etc. So I sit on the bench most of the season until our coach finally put me in a game. I start out well, zip in front of my opponent, grab the ball, and streak down the floor for an easy lay-up basket. The small crowd cheers.

Unfortunately as I go up for that basket, I get nervous and miss. The crowd groans. But I get my own rebound so the crowd cheers again. Then I go up with a second lay-up and miss again. The crowd groans again. The coach pulls me out and I sit on the bench for the remainder of the season.

This is what life can be like for us humans in the early stages of Coping Skills. Everything becomes an ordeal of learning with repeated *trial and error* as we try to improve our coping skill, whether learning to play basketball, drive cars, play chess, or get dates with whomever.

My experience may remind you own early Coping Skills. *Goals are different, but the game is the same. Learn from Experience to move up in the world.* In that process we usually make lots more mistakes than animals. At least I did. How about you? How was the first time you kissed someone outside your family?

Stage 3 is *Competence. Rules are no longer needed: you are used to things. Experience is now the primary teacher, and with enough of it, competence results.* Our intentions become useful instead of embarrassing. We feel our way and we learn how to deal with different situations in different ways. Eventually we become *Competent*.

My raccoon friend and I feel our way along too, although we are playing different positions as we adjust to the game. Neither of us are missing lay-ups.

Then she arrives one day with three friends, possibly peers from her covey, and I face the problem of whether to provide enough food for all four of them. By now I have enough Competence to adjust by feeding her in *her* bowl and the others in a second bowl in which I gradually slow down the food until eventually she is the only one showing up most of the time.

She cooperates beautifully. *If* they try to intrude onto *her* bowl, she *copes* by snapping at them with her sharp teeth, often making them squeal and run away. So the intruders learn the same way I did in junior high, the hard way, that some things are not cut out for us. My raccoon friend and I demonstrate our mutual *Competence through Experience*.

Stage 4 is Proficiency, a deeper level of Experience. Dreyfus describes it as the level where when driving on a rain drenched road you "decide" without thinking whether to let up or lean on accelerator and/or brakes.

I was clearly not ready for the next stage on the slippery road of raccoon care the next year, although my raccoon friend handles her complexities in an admirable way.

One night she shows up with four exceptionally cute baby raccoons following faithfully behind *her* in a row. Not exactly the same rodeo as with Momma Bear with her cub. It is fascinating to watch her Maternal Instincts at work, especially her treatment of what some today would call her "special child", whose growth and behavior during coming months continues to lag seriously behind the others.

She seems to operate "spontaneously and without thought", as Dreyfus' describes Proficiency, to know how to deal with her special child. She is way beyond the Novice, Advanced Beginner, and even Competent stage.

What impresses me first is when she appears to *gesture* with her right front leg and paw for her very timid special child to come to *her* bowl, while the others have to eat at *their bowl*. She uses a very different technique than I had seen with her "friends" the year before. I kid you not. She treats her special child differently.

Her special child learns eventually to answer her beckoning and come to *her* bowl, usually after the others have emptied and left their own bowl and gone off to climb my young peach tree, break off some limbs, and eat most of the peaches. I finally shot all of them.

No, I don't really shoot them. You know how us soft father types can be. We sometimes talk big, but beneath it all we are pussycats. Besides, I didn't lose all *that* many limbs and peaches.

If her other pups dare to come to her bowl as they grow up, she just pushes them away rather than snaps at them as she had the older raccoons the year before, but still she allows no intrusions into her bowl, except for her special child.

It gradually comes to me that what I'd earlier taken to be peers from her covey were probably her nearly grown-up brood of pups from the year before. *In any case, Momma Raccoon rates as a Proficiently skilled momma in child raising.* Agreed?

I show Competency again in slowly applying the brakes on the cat food as I had the year before, but I am a failure with my peach tree. They don't break off many limbs, but they eventually get almost all of my peaches.

After her other children apparently leave home for life on their own, Momma Raccoon continues to appear with her special child for a long time. She no longer needs to coax it to her bowl, and she does not snap like she did at the its kin when they tried to push their way into her bowl, etc.

When I start making a separate bowl for her special child, she seems occasionally to politely nudge her special child out of the way to go back to its own bowl until she was finished, and then allows it to have whatever is left hers if needed. Her special child's behavior has improved, but not enough to imagine it could function on its own. Ever known a kid like that?

Then there is nothing to be seen of either of them for a long time. Then one night she appears again, fat and sassy. I know it is her because she comes up to me with that old "Where is my cat food" look, but there is no sign of any pups. A week or two later what is obviously her special child appears alone, and I gesture to it the same way her momma appeared to do earlier, and it finally comes to the bowl.

After a few weeks of this, the special child disappears, and since then I have seen neither special child nor Momma Raccoon. The raccoons who come now are very late at night. I only assume they have been here by the missing cat food in the morning.

Stage 5 is *Expertise, the deepest of all levels of Coping Skills.* To Dreyfus this is the level of a chess master who quietly and spontaneously considers thousands of possible moves in the few moments allowed in championship tournaments, and makes the right move. We will return to this stage in Part 2. The goal so far is understand how coping skills are learned directly through Experience, no matter how much Experience it takes.

What happens when a computer finally "defeats" a chess champion? There is no question about whether human or computer has a better and quicker memory and can "memorize" every conceivable play, etc. That is one of several reasons I love my computer. The more it can do for me the more I love it.

But why should I want to compete with it? If it wants to fight with me, I can use one of my other tools, a hammer, and smash it, but why would I want to do that when it is a very important tool and big part of me and my life?

As for Momma Raccoon, she surely warrants Proficiency status, if not Expertise, but I am not sure how you measure Expertise for a raccoon.

I think I have Proficiency as a human parent. I have had half the parental responsibility in raising four incredible grown-up daughters to whom I have dedicated this book.

Could it be that I am a soft touch for them, too? Perhaps, but they don't climb my little peach tree, break its limbs, and eat all my peaches, so they are much easier at this point in life to deal with, bless their hearts.

SCENE 7
HONEYBEES: COMMUNITY LIFE

For both animals and humans Life is rarely life alone. In fact there is no species if there is only one individual in it, right? One mistake that *Darwin made is that despite his evolutionary theories, he was still a child of the scientific age before him and preoccupied with survival of the "fittest", meaning superior, rather than able to fit with their social and physical environment. Granting that what fits may change with the times, without lots of good fits, any species is doomed.*

We all know competition is important, because it too *fits* in its own way, but if you are the only one left standing in competition, you are standing alone, and that means the end of you unless you learn to collaborate one way or another. Complex Systems theories make that clear today.

A socially Complex System survives only as long as it keeps moving organically and manages to maintain enough equilibrium to survive and prosper. Evolution does that for a living.

Communal life varies widely from one species to another. For us that may not require 20 million humans in a single building, as with the bats in Bracken Cave in Texas between March and October. Nor does it require a neighborhood with even 50 thousand humans in a single building, as in the three honeybee hives in my back yard when I lived in Michigan. *All species, including us, require living together in order to survive and prosper. Once when Life was relatively simple, perhaps brute power could provide this from the top down, but for humans, no longer.*

Of course reproduction helps. Earthworms and paramecia self-produce. We can't, but we have more complex and interesting ways of doing it, right? But some species over-populate themselves out of existence, including us if we are not careful.

Bees are a fascinating illustration of a wonderfully manageable society. Theirs is not for us of course, but for them it has worked for eons quite well. Moreover, they pollinate enormous numbers of plants we depend on, from clover fields to fruit trees, and the honey we eat sometimes instead of strawberry preserves with peanut butter in our sandwiches.

Midland, Michigan was a wonderful place to live, populated by Dow personnel whose environmental concerns made it a safe place for bees to live without insecticides and herbicides. Murrieta is OK, but I find too many dead bees in my swimming pool to feel safe having bees here, at least so far, although I am working on it. As what I usually call "a good person", I am trying to educate our city fathers about bees. It takes more than my neighbors; a bee hive needs a *huge* neighborhood.

In Michigan I began my adventure with bees by buying all the usual necessities, a kit to build a beehive, a small colony of bees, the usual processing equipment for transferring the honey from honeycomb to bottle, and the usual protection, a screened hat so they could not get to my face and gloves for my hands. I was too stingy to buy the entire suit for the job. Soon I stopped using even the hat and gloves, foolish as usual concerning my ability to take care of myself.

For a few years my non-protection worked well. I even captured the first of two swarms as they left the old hive to find a new one, and eventually had three hives. I learned they usually make their first stopping point a nearby limb while scouting bees search for a good location for a new home.

So I first took off the lid and entry of the locked hive that had been ready for a quite a while, went over and cut off the limb where the swarm of thousands of bees gathered around the queen, and carried it over to the now *unlocked* hive I had waiting for them. Beekeeping is an adventure, but as a hypoglycemic, I am automatically a good friend of honey as well as bees.

It was quite an adventure carrying across the yard a huge blob of bees wrapped around the queen, but I knew they rarely sting while swarming, and they didn't. Both times I did this during the years we lived there, they took my suggestion and moved quickly into the empty hive, where they immediately went to work.

Bees always overproduce honey, which is how we humans get some too. It was fun taking the frames of honey into the garage to extract the honey. With the help of a "smoker" to calm them when I opened the hive and they allowed me to take the top frames of the hives, leaving the bottom larger frames for them.

I, like all beekeepers, placed a grid which will allow workers to pass, but not the much larger queen to lay her eggs except in the lower cells of the hive. Below the grid it made a good place for baby bees to gestate and other bees to have honey for meals.

I kept the human share of the honey in different jars for the different flavors in different parts of the season. Clover fields make the light honey you probably prefer; back yard honey is usually darker and richer, depending on blooms at the time.

The bees and I were not only friends but connoisseurs of honey in those days. Perhaps you see why I miss my bees.

However, as I am sitting near one of the hives one day reading a book, without looking I swat at what I think is a fly on my left fore-arm and it is a honeybee, who does her bee duty and stings me, considering me a threat to the hive. I had never been stung by a bee that I can recall.

Honeybees usually sting only when they, their hive, or their friends are under attack and they are very dangerous to humans if bees nearby get an attack message through the air. Then every bee nearby suddenly follows suit.

They all do this very unselfishly, realizing that they die soon after stinging you, suddenly missing an essential part of their bodies, but they are unafraid to sacrifice their lives. They resemble the Navy Seals in *Tears of the Sun* in Part 3.

It only requires one bee, however, to knock me out of commission. I have enough sense to go inside the house, where I notice that although it does not hurt, the little bump is swelling and doesn't stop. When it gets to my shoulder, I head for the hospital emergency room, and the discovery that without knowing it, I'm very allergic to honeybee stings. If I waited any longer. I might have died.

The doctor injects me with whatever and the swelling slowly begins to go down. He presents me with two alternatives, (1) get rid of my bees or (2) sign up for an extensive program of shots that will immunize me. Jesse asks what would happen if I did neither.

He says next time I get stung it would (1) be even worse if I do not have time to get to the hospital, or (2) it might not bee as bad because my body might start to develop its own immunity program.

What would you do? Foolish Jesse asks for a third alternative. The doctor balks at first, but then admits says he could give me a bee-sting kit I would *probably* get to the hospital in time. Well, you know foolish Jesse. He takes that option and is not stung again for years.

This time I don't even have to use the kit. The sting on my right forearm doesn't even swell up as far as my elbow. I haven't been stung since, and assume I'm no longer allergic to honeybees.

So I look before I leap in swatting "flies", but do not resist honeybees landing on me accidentally. They just walk around a bit, take off, and I wave goodbye.

Queen Bee is actually a misnomer. As the only fertile female in the hive, she is actually more slave than queen. She lays thousands upon thousands of eggs and is treated well only to maintain the population.

Embodiment

Human queens obviously don't have to do that. They usually just sit around dressed in beautiful clothes and jewels.

However, the queen bee is the only one in the hive who experiences sex and lives to tell the tale. Worker bees (supposedly) are forever immature females. The only male bees are the Drones, the only other bees larger than Workers.

Like some men, they just hang around the house waiting for the female workers to bring home the bacon, so to speak, and feed them. The only useful thing Drones do is fertilize the queen on her rare maiden flights. Reminds me of roosters.

Drones just cruise the boulevard looking for sex. Remind you of anybody you know? If any drone is a lucky one and gets to mate with a queen on her rare day off while drones are out carousing, "it" may happen above the tree tops during an acrobatic ritual dance in the sky, at the end of which they fall to the ground literally bound together. Very romantic, right?

That could be, except that at the end she pulls off part of his essentials and he dies. So I hope it was good. She flies back to the hive and lays thousands and thousands of eggs till it is time to fly again.

I doubt most women would like to trade places with a queen bee, but it does have its attractions. Would any of you women agree? Or would you rather follow the old Hollywood classics, and just share a cigarette together, etc.?

Why am I getting so many details? So you can learn how honeybee culture is a Dynamic Complex System in which every player has a role to play, and does so without questioning it. Like human cultures, a bee hive has roles and rituals.

Honeybee hives are built from long term *Habits*, as C. S. Peirce would call them, habits that have survived well for ages. We as humans should be so successful. Honeybees even have a language of sorts, which I will describe later in the book.

We also *develop and keep good Habits that actually work, so we naturally keep them as long as they continue to work.*

*A*pparently today some hives have worker bees that are fertile, so even bee hives have exceptions and rebels. Our *Habits* seem to change much more rapidly, also resulting unanticipated risks.

Our efforts to develop good cultural habits will be described in Scene 7 of Part 2 and in more detail in all the Scenes of Parts 3 and 4. I have intentionally described here habits that parallel human culture, the territory into which we enter at the end of Part 2.

Some human customs are similar to those of bees, others are different. *All cultures, animal or human, but cultural habits in any case become experientially tested and embodied.* More about both bees and humans in Part 2, Scene 7, but first another movie.

Ready for that? If not, take a break. There is no rush.

PART 2

INSTINCT
SPECTRE

The subject in Part 1 was *"what comes to us"*, which often arises spontaneously and surprisingly in everyday Experience. *Part 2 begins with Instinct. What "comes to us" comes from even deeper roots that are traditionally called Instincts.*

Instincts are defined in most dictionaries as innate, unlearned, and fixed patterns of behavior. The case made in this book is that all Instincts are alive, growing, and learning processes from the bottom up, and very unfixed from the very beginning. Only warped forms of Instincts are innate, unlearned, and fixed patterns of behavior.

Sexual and Killer instincts originate in primal living instincts of Pleasure and Pain. These origins are as old as evolutionary history itself, but traditional definitions of them are like saying there are letters in the alphabet, ignoring that the alphabet is Alive and Open Ended.

The philosophical roots of Instincts in this book go back to C. S. Peirce. Peirce focuses first on how virtually all of reality in one way or another is Dynamic and Alive as described in both *Youniverse* 2020 and in *Embodiment* 2020. More recently Maurice Merleau-Ponty says the same kind of things about Experience and Perception.

Peirce is also focused of how humans *fit* together *within* their community, while Darwin is into survival of the *fittest* in rising *above* competitors in order to lead their clan to triumph.

To Peirce Love Instinct is on one side of what fits and the Killer Instinct on the other. Both are Active Instincts historically in human struggles to Survive, but the question is: How can they Fit together, if at all.

Bond's basic orientation in the four films with Daniel Craig playing Bond revolves first on his *Killer Instinct*, which is basic to his 007 status in the British intelligence agency M 16. Bond is famous for the many villains he kills, but he is also famous for his many lovers. He moves smoothly from killing villains one moment and love affairs the next. *He triumphs over evil as the playboy of the western world. Love and Killer Instincts never really clash.*

However, in the four Daniel Craig movies they do clash, and Bond struggles with this. *First, the next paragraphs begin quickly with Spectre, because that is where Bond actually uses the term Instinct, but in a very non-traditional way if you look at it carefully.*

Spectre begins with a new M (Ralph Fiennes), director of M 16, the strategic home of Double O agents like 007 Bond. The earlier M (Judy Dench) has died at the end of *Sky Fall*. The new M explains to an associate that Double O agents have *permission* rather than *order* to kill. So much for the Killer Instinct as a fixed *"package"*.

Early in the movie, Bond asks Moneypenny, the usually faithful assistant to M, to help him as a "mole" (going underground for secret information the way moles *sniff* out its prey, rather than *hear* them like bats). She asks what makes him think she will do this when it could jeopardize not only her job but her life. He answers with one word: *Instinct*.

We will explore the more detailed context for this event later, but it is already obvious that this is neither his sexual or killer instincts at work. Bond is not exploiting her sexual instincts as he has in early Bond movies, because Moneypenny in contrast to her predecessors does not dream of a romance with Bond. The new Moneypenny of *Skyfall* and *Spectre* (Naomie Harris) is very different from her earlier "embodiments". She feels a very different kind of bond with Bond. His interesting name will be explored later.

Yet he simply answers her question with that simple *Instinct*. Why would he say this? Consider this: Bond's gradually developing instincts in Daniel Craig's Bond movies could be described as what neuroscientist Antonio Damasio calls *Supra-Instinctive Survival Strategies*. What Bond means here is definitely *not* Instinct as an "innate and unlearned" package.

The early phenomenologist Edmund Husserl said that consciousness is consciousness (of), one way of saying that conscious is fluid rather than static, always *moving* into the future. The later German phenomenologist Martin Heidegger insists that *Consciousness is fluid from bottom to top. Heidegger wants to go below the detached knower to an involved doer*. So what?

First consider Joe Black's Instinctual Development not only from Disembodiment to Embodiment, but from Empathy to Compassion. We find the dynamics of *Individual* Empathy and Compassion in the *Spectre* series. We will come back to *Soci*al Empathy in Scene 7 and carry that on into Parts 3 and 4.

So for now bracket off *Spectre* in order to place it in the context of all four Daniel Craig movies as Bond. The four movies, with ups and downs, show a *gradual Decline of his Killer Instinct and a Incline of his Instinctive Empathy and Compassion*. That theme seems to run toward *Spectre* from *Casino Royale*, *Quantum of Solace*, and *Skyfall*.

His first brief romance in *Casino Royale* begins with the traditional Bond model; Alternating triumphs in battle with spending time in bed with a beautiful woman, in this case the wife of the man he just killed, but then she didn't seem to be grieving much.

When he later meets Vesper, however, their relationship is very different. This time the movie does not end with a scandalized M suddenly finding him celebrating his triumph in bed with his latest flame.

As their relationship deepens, Vesper asks him why he continues in such grim work, and the question seems to soak in for him as they survive several threatening ordeals together.

Then, completely out of character for Bond, he falls in love with her, promises to love her unconditionally, and leave his Killer-Instinct job behind. *But* then he learns that she is returning his rescued money to the forces of evil. He tries to save her during a violent battle, but she drowns. He's left alone, holding her body in his arms.

Still feeling betrayed by her leads to what is often called *Reaction Formation*, a defense mechanism where everything is turned backward. He tells M (played by Judy Dench in first three Craig-Bond movies): "The Bitch is dead." She surprises him by telling him that Vesper actually died trying to save his life. Bond seems somewhat touched, but aggressively returns to his work,

In this scene, however, M herself becomes emotionally more interesting, as we shall see later in *Skyfall*. She had earlier come across as rather heartless, but in her effort to correct Bond's reaction to Vesper's death, she appears rather maternal. She like Bond seems to be learning things.

In *Quantum of Solace*, Bond expresses his reaction to Vesper's death through *Revenge* on the mastermind he thinks responsible for Vesper's death. He leaves him alone in the middle of a barren desert with only a can of oil to drink and is found dead later, the oil can dry and with unexplained bullets in his head.

This appears to demonstrate that Revenge is Sweet. But *Quantum* in the title may among other things suggest this is only *part* of the *Solace* needed for Vesper's death.

Skyfall brings us back to Bond's and M's emotional maturation. Bond's birth parents had died early in his life. M's temperament picks up where it ends in *Casino Royal*, as a quasi-mother.

The final battle takes place on Bond's childhood estate, now abandoned except for its fatherly caretaker. Bond, M, and the caretaker fight off the villains, a classic battle of Defending the Homestead. The homestead however is virtually destroyed while Bond becomes emotionally more involved with his quasi-mother M.

In the wreckage of the estate M dies at his side in a touching scene. This is very different from other Bond movies, and *Skyfall* is surprisingly a box office success beyond the earlier Craig Bond films.

The plot of *Spectre* begins in Mexico with a "death come to life" festival. Bond escapes what seems like "certain death" several times, ending with a dramatic struggle in a helicopter as it swoops down near the awestruck festival crowd below, then up rolling upside down while he and his foe fight, hanging to the copter. He eventually boots both his foe and the pilot out the door, takes the controls, skims over the crowd below, and flies away home.

The new M (Ralph Fiennes) is now *his aloof father surrogate*. When Bond tells the new M that he was in Mexico for a vacation, M harshly tells him he is grounded and has lost all his privileges. However, Bond coerces Q, the young technical expert, to provide him access to a very high tech and expensive car by threatening to harm his cats. He then meets with Moneypenny in his apartment.

Here is his famous dialogue with Moneypenny. Although she is quite attractive, Bond treats her more like a younger sister in his family, which may be part of why she trusts him when he says: "Instinct".

She agrees to be his "mole". She has already been close to Bond in earlier episodes, more as *a younger sister* than a *would-be lover*. She and Q, the young genius technology expert, are both treated like younger family members.

Bond usually has to trick or manipulate Q into collaborating, as he might a *much younger brother*. Moneypenny needs no manipulation nor does Q by the end of the movie. *By then the Family is together*.

Back to Moneypenny, he has also obviously forgiven her for once nearly killing him by shooting on M's order when Bond was struggling with a culprit on top of a train about to go into a tunnel and instead she hits Bond, who appears at first to die in a long fall off the train and into the raging river the train is passing, but of course we later learn he survives.

Have you ever forgiven someone in your family who tried but failed to save your rear end? He or she at least tried, right?

Bond sets up *his older brother role* with Moneypenny by confiding *a secret of his own*: he has been acting since *Skyfall* on a secret tape left behind somehow by M, asking him to pursue a clue from the ring Bond slips off the culprit's hand before he falls from the helicopter. That ring is the next clue M wants him to pursue to reach the man who has been ordering nefarious international acts.

When Moneypenny asks how he got this tape, he replies that M does not let something like death keep her from doing her work.

The ring points him in time to a cabin in Austria. There he discovers Mr. White (names are often interesting in Bond films), dying from poisoning by the evil mastermind to whom Bond has been led by the "dead" M.

Now, I ask you: What do you suppose M now *really* means in these Donald Craig Bond movies? If you don't know, ask your mother what the first letter of mother is.

Embodiment

Mr. White had earlier worked for Hannes Oberhauser (a slightly Germanized name suggesting one who "rules over the house"). How- ever, Mr. White's "conscience has grown" when Oberhauser began planning *Genocidal* acts, including slaughtering women and children during his power grabs. (We come again to Genocide in Part 3. Now aren't you happy you didn't get ahead of yourself and jump to the end?)

Meanwhile Bond's own conscience has grown, for as he feels *Empathy* for the suffering of Mr. White, and *Compassion* when he promises to protect the life of his daughter, who also turns out to be the next clue to Oberhauser's location.

When Bond finds her, he immediately has to rescue her in a madcap pursuit through the mountains. Their relationship, which is central to the rest of the movie, is similar yet different from his relationship with Vesper in *Casino Royale*.

Unlike Vesper, Madeleine is temperamentally much more like Bond. She too has lived without a father since childhood, separated and unable to reveal her identity because of her father and his earlier role with Oberhauser. She seems aloof and unemotional in rebuffing his dramatic saving of her life. Unlike women in his earlier movies, she also rebuffs any romantic inclinations he may have in mind.

She slowly warms to him, however, as Vesper did, during their pursuit for the man responsible for her father's death. *As in Joe Black, dealing with death together with someone else can be downright redemptive and "Bonding".*

During a private dinner on a train to their next destination, Madeleine asks similar questions to those Vesper had asked him: What he would do if he ever left his dreadful profession of killing people and always being hunted?

However, dinner is interrupted when a fierce and brutal henchman of Oberhauser bursts in and starts knocking Bond around, and a violent struggle ensues. Madeline engages in the fight first with a club and then with a gun, but only manages to wound the brute in the arm.

As the brute is strangling her, Bond gets a rope around his neck from behind. The rope is attached to heavy barrels, so when the first barrels are kicked toward the open train door, they drag the rest of the barrels together with the brute out the door.

Guess what happens next? Bond and Madeleine finally end up in bed. He pledges his love to her, again saying he will retire from the Secret Service, just as he had with Vesper.

But Bond's family history plot is growing even thicker. We learn why Oberhauser is so intent in destroying everything dear to Bond. Brace yourself for this if you have not already seen the movie:

Oberhauser is actually Bond's insanely jealous foster-brother who had killed his own father long ago during the avalanche that supposedly killed them both. His father had always favored Bond over him when they were young. In his maniacal jealousy and *Genocidal Revenge*, he claims he has been behind the death of all women in Bond's adult life, including Vesper and M his quasi-mother, etc.

Oberhauser is the epitome of Social Solipsism, to which we will return in Part 3. Now he can take complete Revenge on Bond, by assuring Bond he has not only killed everyone dear to Bond, he is completing his plan to destroy the entire British Secret Service, after he lobotomizes Bond before killing him and Madeleine, his last love. In the desert with motor oil is paltry Revenge compared to this, agreed?

Tied and bound during the procedure, it looks like Bond's non-Canadian goose is cooked, so to speak, but he manages to slip his incendiary watch to Madeleine and she tosses it toward Oberhauser and it goes off. In the following melee they destroy the internet hub of

Oberhauser's extensive conclave, and escape by helicopter. It looks like Oberhauser is dead, but as Bond remarks, this is not over yet.

When he and Madeleine reach London, Oberhauser's agent C has taken over the Secret Service and is now dismantling the power of the new M, who *like all good surrogate fathers* is not taking this lying down. So as a family evident so to speak, M, Q, and Moneypenny are competing against C, who falls to his death in a fight with M.

Meanwhile, however, Oberhauser has somehow survived the destruction of his citadel, kidnapped Madeleine, who has been attempting to remove herself from all this, and has her tied and bound at the top of the building that once housed the old Double O program, scheduled for destruction in 3 minutes. As the building collapses Bond and Madeleine escape in a speedboat, pursuing Oberhauser's escaping helicopter.

Bond manages finally to fire into the heavily armed helicopter's exhaust outlets and brings it slowly down. It crashes on top of a bridge, and Bond climbs up from the boat and stands with his gun pointed at his wounded foster-brother, who tells Bond to "finish it". *Now*, recall what M told his colleague early in the movie about Double O agents.

Bond, aware of his alternatives, discharges the cartridge on the ground, and says that he is out of shells. He then announces that he has something better to do. He leaves Oberhauser to M. Tossing his pistol aside, he walks away toward Madeline, who stands awaiting him.

At the end of the movie, having left his Killer Instincts behind, they are driving off together in the restored car Bond has used in early Bond movies, which his good younger brother type Q had restored for him (without having now to threaten Q's cats). Up an urban street instead of toward the sunset but in good Hollywood fashion, they leave all the ordeals behind.

When Craig is asked later about further Bond movies, perhaps in part because Craig suffered serious injuries making Bond movies, he says he would rather slit his wrists on a nearby piece of glass than do another. Case closed. Apparently, there will be no more Bond movies, although rumor has it that Craig has been offered 150 million dollars to do another.

However, I now hear he will soon be doing that.

PART 2
SCENE 1 FROM EMPATHY TO COMPASSION

"I see what you mean", "I hear what you are saying", "I feel for you","What a sweet idea", and "I smell a rat in that theory" are *not* just figures of speech. *Like other animals, we see, hear, feel, taste, and even smell our way along everywhere we go.*

Forget about killer and other aggressive instincts for now. Let's begin with the origins of *Empathy*, our feeling of basic *Identification* with other humans and/or Life in general.

What is happening in Part I when the pigs and I relate to each other? How does one neurological system relate to another before even having words and language to do that?

Walter Freeman, one of the few neurologists to say much about this sort of thing, sees a *resonance* of sorts between neurological systems that adds up to a sense of each other as similar beings, the kind of recognition we might add that occurs in the first *real* look you take at your mommy.

What do you suppose a mother sees when she looks into her new baby's eyes? She may not stop to think about this, and certainly her baby doesn't, but they look back at each other in a way that *Bonds* them together. You are *my* mommy, I am *your* mother, or some such thing in a non-verbal language. You both pick up a *resonance*. You *sense* it.

You may have noticed how quickly a new baby can distinguish Mom from other people, and soon other people from each other, not just by sight but by sound, feeling, and even smell. It is only takes a little time for a baby to look into a mirror and see a self-image, not some other baby.

You take these for granted now, right? Well, once you did not, but you don't recall that. I'm sure my mother and I started the same way, but the first thing I actually remember is the pig-wallow episode. I should add in case you wonder that I actually identify much more with my mother than pigs. I just don't remember that.

It is difficult to imagine exactly what either the pigs sensed in me or I in them. I can imagine that they saw me as a poor little pig with a somewhat distorted body who needs a family, or that I saw them as a family that, unlike the one I left behind in the house, loved dirt. My recollection may be off a bit, but it was probably something like that, although in my mind's eye I recall it in color, sound, and most of all, feel of the mud and pigs. I don't recall the smell, but mud is *not*, like poop, all that smelly if you don't already know this.

Whatever it was for me, some kind of *Identity* was there, as I was welcomed into the pig-wallow as one of them. There we were, one nice pig family having fun, until my mom saw what we were doing, and tried her best by demands and threats to convince me that I was not a pig. Over time she more or less succeeded.

Appearances of course can be deceiving in determining who we *really* are. Actors and actresses make a living on that. Most politicians and sales people are not very good at it, but they try. However, actors and actresses are not very good trying at convincing me for whom I should vote. Unfortunately they usually come across as amateurish sales people trying to sell used cars. Perhaps they should just stay with movies and music.

This is why I often ask students and now you to look at people around you and ask yourself: Can I imagine myself buying a used car from this person? Fortunately, we still have a more or less reliable sense of who the other person really is just by *looking* at them. We Psychotherapists make a living doing that kind of thing. It sometimes tells me more than psychological tests. It pays to have Good Sense.

Walter Freeman describes what he calls the Complications of Solipsism, those who only experience themselves, not others.

Embodiment

That easily becomes *Solipsistic Isolationism.* Know anybody like that in Spectre?

Each of us however is unique. Although there are billions of us on earth, no two of us are identical. Do you know any "identical" twins? Are they really identical? If they have different lives, they are not identical. You are not interchangeable with anyone else anywhere. *You are the only one of you on earth, yet you feel kinship with others.* Strange, isn't it?

Intimate relationships are as close as we come to each other, but even intimate relationships do not make two people completely identical. Folks where I come from often describe their spouses as their "better half", which is understandable. Some couples may come close, but they are at least somewhat different from each other.

Different, and yet the same, or at least similar. What makes it possible for you to relate to me as you read this book when you can't even see me?

Freeman raises a great question when he asks: What is the neurological response to meeting another creature of our kind? This is when Solipsism Isolation can be like a baby looking at Others is like looking into a mirror and seeing oneself.

How do we maintain our own identity and yet relate to others as Others rather than as extensions of ourselves. Where and how do we start when we meet someone for the first or any other time?

Socrates never asked this kind of question so far as I know. Like traditional scientists who focus on objective matter, he started much farther up the line than the Senses when asking questions. No wonder he couldn't understand an expert on pious experiences.

Perhaps he should have started his investigations with his mother. Tradition has it that she was a mid-wife. Consider again a mother looking into her baby's eyes or the baby looking back. What do they see in each other's eyes?

Time begins to distinguish the images, that they are not "singular" but "similar", as with little Jesse sitting in the mud-wallow looking into the eyes of his pig friends. Complicated, isn't it?

I mean, what do you see when you look into the eyes of a pet? What would you guess your pet sees?

Freeman proposes we understand such things as a kind of *resonance* of neurological vibrations *but* one that is somewhat different without losing the Identity. That makes sense, doesn't it?

But for Oberhauser in *Spectre* that resonance never seems to click. He seems locked solipsistically inside himself, detached from the world around him, which he resents. No wonder his cat goes to sit on Bond's lap. He just takes the cat off before he tries to lobotomize Bond.

Looking into Oberhauser's eyes is like looking into the eyes of a grizzly who doesn't really look angry, just that it is looking for the best way to have you for dinner. Even a grizzly bear mom may look in a different way at her cub, but Oberhauser has no children and no real relationships with anyone, not even his father, whom he killed for loving his foster-brother more than him. Is he impressed favorably when Bond spares him at the end of Spectre? How will he deal with his approaching imprisonment?

Empathy is also somewhat lacking at first in James Bond, except for the vestiges of family relationships before his life as a double 0 agent, where he develops a Bond a family relationship of sorts with his compatriots in the Secret Service, especially as they develop in the four movies. The family table is set for him by the time he meets Madeleine.

Embodiment

The big difference between Bond and his foster-brother shows up when he begins to have trouble killing people when he feels Empathy for Mr. White, he hands his own gun to him as *proof* that he is serious about saving his daughter's life.

Empathy is where we all start. It is our first test in Life. If we pass, we build from there. If we continue to fail the tests, we lose the ability to separate numbers from nerves. More about numbers and nerves later.

If Empathy is missing, a mother teaching anything to her child in the absence of Empathy would be like teaching a child how to walk without legs and feet or how to build buildings without blocks.

As C. S. Peirce suggests, everything starts with *things*, which become signs, which become words, etc. A Harvard professor recently dismissed *Empathy* as unimportant compared to *Rational Compassion*. That is what we Hoosiers call "putting the cart before the horse".

No one in their right mind believes that Compassion, whether rational or not, is enough all by itself. *Complex Systems are Alive.* Disembodied so-called "compassion" is not. Put the cart in front of the horse and the cart keeps running off the road. Go figure.

Now go back to Bond. If you have seen any of the four Craig/Bond movies, you know early on that his eyes don't exactly sparkle, except when in the presence of a beautiful woman. Look at Moneypenny. She has real eyes. Hers remind me of Bonnie's eyes; they sparkle like the eyes of a child.

Most of us lose something of that as we grow older. Time does tend to dull the sparkle of our senses. Just look around. What do you see in others, or perhaps in the mirror?

Life of course can be hard. No wonder Bond's eyes do not sparkle often. If you lost your parents early in life and since then killed and/ or saw killed as many people as he has, or spent as much time playing poker as he has, your eyes wouldn't sparkle much either. It is difficult to keep eyes bright, right?

But when your eyes sparkle, they can make a difference. When Moneypenny is around, Bond's light up a little, and it is not sexual attraction doing it for a change. Moneypenny is one of the few beautiful women for whom he seems to have no romantic feelings, yet inspire him. Who is she to him?

Lots of people's eyes don't sparkle much. Sometimes there are understandable reasons for that. Consider poker players, for example, like Bond at the card table. If they get a hand that is full of aces, you don't see their eyes sparkling, or if they are, it will be the only hand they will ever win. But of course it is more fun for Bond to go to bed with someone than play poker. His eyes sparkle more there.

Bond never develops eyes like Moneypenny's, but he does have a different glint in his eyes when he leaves his un-sparkling foster-brother on the ground and turns toward Madeleine at the end of *Spectre*. He may not be a world champion eye-sparkler like Moneypenny, nor is Madeleine for that matter, but as I said before, Madeleine is more his speed.

As they drive away "into the sunset" at the end of the movie, they both sparkle more than they did early in the movie.

Recall the pig with glasses photo beside my desk that I described earlier? Even pigs can have a certain sparkle in their eyes. Our human identity shows in many different ways, as do our expressions.

So "I *see* what you mean", "I *hear* what you are saying", etc. are not just figures of speech, as stated at the beginning of this scene. Our senses are at the heart of things for all of us, even if we are fairly good at hiding them

Would you agree?

PART 2
SCENE 2 THE NEUROLOGY OF EMOTION

Single-celled creatures have emotions 0f sorts, as described earlier, but they do not have neurons to the extent we do. A very large symphony orchestra, or if you prefer a rock concert, is performing constantly inside our bodies all the time.

Even insects, however, have lots of neurons. Honeybees have nearly 1,000,000 neurons, pretty impressive for a small insect. Human neurological systems have 100,000,000,000 give or take depending on sources you consult. Only elephants and sea mammals may have that many, but they unfortunately are unable to type on a computer keyboard. All this in any case makes a 2,000 piece puzzle seem like nothing.

What occurs when a human baby is born resembles what occurs when a baby chick hatches and suddenly moves from inside into the outside world. Neurons have a new kind of job to do, but ours is a much bigger one.

A single neuron is like a tree with synapses growing out like tree limbs. An average neuron has as many as 100 such limbs. Multiply that by the numbers of neurons you have and you get a rough idea of the number of connections you have inside this tree of trees in your neurological system.

The most important feature of that system is the intricate balancing act between and among multitudes of neurons. As Walter Freeman, Antonio Damasio, Andy Clark, and others point out, it is amazing how the very structure of our neurological system *anticipates* how we function both individually and socially.

Neurons interact in *populations* with each other that suggest the collective rhythms of dance, music, and other known and cultivated complex practices. I know this from graduate studies in historians of religion like Rudolf Otto, Gerardus van der Leeuw, and more recently Mircea Eliade, all of whom wrote about the colorful rituals of primal cultures.

Neurobiology adds support to early 20th century historians, phenomenologists, and anthropologists in their understanding of *Intentionality*, the heart of all consciousness. It goes even deeper than the collective Unconscious of Carl Jung, or the Psychosocial stages of Erik Erickson. Everyone is now undergirded, corrected, and/or supplemented in neurological ways that make ever more complex sense.

Antonio Damasio's best-known book on Rene Descartes (1994) and his book on Baruch Spinoza (2003) are basic to several issues in this book. They have become classics for *Embodied Cognitive Science*, including more recently Andy Clark, whose works are listed in Recommended Books.

The neurological "tree" continues things with branches and "leaves" interacting with surroundings and becoming ever more complex. Areas of Interactive emotional development, for example, can move intricately from fear to anxiety and/or from anger to rage.

Fear, blended with *Sadness* and *Submission*, may become *Embarrassment*, *Shame*, and *Guilt*. *Disgus*t and Anger may become Contempt and Indignation. *Attachment and Sadness may become Sympathy and Compassion.* You see such things happening in Bond's maturation in the four movies.

I grow a hundred Caladium bulbs every year. Go to that site on the internet and you will see what I mean. No two colorful leaves are identical, especially in the most beautiful varieties. Every leaf can be a meditation object, as can every day in the life of you and your neurons.

Primal emotions like *Pain* and *Pleasure* are without consequences until you leave the egg like a little chick and enter the outside world There you evolve from sources that have been formulated carefully over eons to help you do that, and as contact takes place, *Pain* and *Pleasure* can begin to develop toward *Sympathy* and *Compassion*.

In other words, the world opens through shaping and reshaping, touching and learning, mimicking the movement from the egg in the shell to the little chick exploring the outer world.

In this process for us humans (1) Background Emotions, (2) Primary Emotions, and (3) Social Emotions emerge, so now we are also into the territory of what Damasio calls *Somatic Markers*.

As I understand them, such Markers" are not just inert "packages" (saying stop, go, or whatever). They are more like *mini-strategies, markers of what works*, since as Damasio says, neurons are always *Minding the Future*. In other words, they are *Dynamic* and *Living*, not *Mechanical* and *Dead*.

With proliferation of experiences, however, there is not only proliferation but condensation of the *Affect/Effects* of these neurons and their markers into practical influences for future problems, which takes place in the *Pre-Frontal Cortex* of the brain.

There Markers can feed into anything from an expression on the face to a quick action, such as Bond saying "*Instinct*", i.e., when experience needs no further processing. It then becomes scaffolding perhaps for further processing in the Frontal Lobes. Mistakes can be made in either place, but that's Life. In time Evolution usually corrects itself.

Neurobiology is becoming integral in a wide variety of fields, including the philosophy of Hubert Dreyfus, whom you met quickly in Part 1, Scene 6. Robert Sapolsky's new 800 page book among many other things supports Damasio's emphasis on Somatic Markers in Decision-Making.

As emotions meander in the direction of Morality, there are sometimes pre-moral combinations as they wander about in some of our *animal forebears*, and strange things can happen. Damasio mentions the *Bonobos*, the "good-natured" apes whose personalities, he says, resemble a marriage of Bill Clinton to Mother Teresa. (That caught your attention didn't it? I am enticing you to read his books if you are up for complex, yet readable books.)

Back to our Scene 1 topic, *Empathy*. As Damasio points out, here emotion moves from (1) *Empathy, feeling the pain* in yourself for someone else who has been injured, to (2) *Sympathy*, feeling *as if you are* the one who is in pain (involvement), and then perhaps (3) *Compassion*, movement toward an *act* to help change things.

This is a very complex processes, which Damasio describes in terms of *Brain States*, which would require too much space here to elaborate technically, but consider a practical illustration from *Spectre* as it unfolds.

Consider first Mr. White slowly dying, poisoned by Oberhauser. Bond (1) *feels* Mr. White's pain" and then reaches toward Mr. White's daughter, deepening his own feelings of (2) *involvement* in the dilemma, which moves then toward (3) *acts* of compassion in saving her (all this sourced by his earlier and slowly developing Compassion in *Skyfall*).

Later in the movie, she will feel the pain of Bond being mauled by the brute, leading toward their collaborative attack of the brute, establishing *Bond's bond* with her. *Now we have the same process occurring in two humans at the same time.*

They learn together (1) what it is like to *feel someone else's pain and* (2) *then becomes their own pain* when Madeleine sees Bond in need of help in his struggle, and (3) goes after the brute with a gun, and gets knocked around herself.

Then Bond pulls himself together and, (1) seeing what is happening to Madeleine, (2) involves himself in the fight and (3) goes after the brute from behind with a rope linked to heavy barrels, the first of which he kicks and the rest fall out the open door of the train, the last dragging the brute out the fast moving train door to his death.

Voila: Mutual Compassion. I mean, life can get really complicated, as you will surely agree, although Mutual Compassion is not discussed such by Damasio.

After all: Why do we go to movies anyway? You may not have experienced anything quite like Bond and Madeleine, and yet in some sense you now have anyway just by seeing the movie, right? We will be on and off this train, so to speak, for the rest of this book.

Think back to M's death scene in *Skyfall*. It is a gripping event. Slowly set up by Bond's trials and tribulations in his early life. Family life can certainly be a complex tangle of overlapping themes. Why do you suppose *Skyfall* was the most popular Bond film to that date?

Has your family history been nothing but a bed or roses? You have not had family experiences quite as dramatic perhaps. Those are just for movies, right? Perhaps you have never had an alcoholic or an addict in your family? Perhaps no one in the family has ever died young? Perhaps no one has ever been seriously injured or had a serious disease? Perhaps no one has ever flunked out of school? Perhaps no one ever gotten a divorce? Never had a pet die? Never prepared a gift for someone and had it ignored? The list is endless, isn't it?

Some of such crises may be "small" crises, if there is such a thing. *The point here is that when emotions come to the surface while watching a movie, they are YOUR feelings and concerns, and no longer just a little old movie.*

It is not just Bond's feelings you are feeling. *Your* feelings during a movie can go right down to your boots and even roots going down from there. You have been there yourself in one way or another perhaps?

Again, why do you go to movies anyway? It may take something outlandish to get your attention, but you have been there already somehow or it would never get to you, right? *I mean, movies are often our pig-wallows. We feel Empathy and we jump in, right?*

Ethics means changing your course and doing something different from that you had been doing, right? Of course Ethics means there is both Good and Bad. Look at Oberhauser. You probably don't know anybody like Oberhauser, and if you do, he wouldn't let you live long enough to tell anyone about it. But nobody is all that bad, right? Let's face it. Chickens also have their problems, but nothing as complex as those we face.

This leads us to the always unfinished conflict between Empathy and Aggression. In the movie that seems resolved when Bond throws away his gun, gets in his classic car with Madeleine and rides into the proverbial sunset.

It also relates to the more somber conclusion of *Tears of the Sun* in Part 3 when Lt. Water flies away with Lena in a helicopter. Both movies describe a gradual movement from Aggression to Empathy to Sympathy to Compassion, which unfortunately provides no easy solution to the conflict where destructive powers of aggression are at stake. Aggression unfortunately never ends.

Suffering never leaves Everywhere. It is the human drama. Where does it leave us? *Things work or they don't, but without basic Empathy, nothing works to solve ethically bad problems.*

What does this have to do with animals? Ask Momma Raccoon. Can you imagine the problem of having a special child?

This is the kind of thing described in upcoming Scenes. All of us have problems of one sort or another. Dealing with them, as in all three movies, Empathy moves toward Compassion, accompanied by Supra-Instinctive Survival Strategies as we go. Eventually we will reach Parts 3 and 4, which concern Cultural Values.

PART 2
SCENE 3 INTENTIONAL GOALS

One difference between us and Canadian geese is that they travel to pretty much the same place every year for their winter vacations, and we don't, although we may do that if we own a time-share agreement where we are going.

We are every bit as *Intentional* as they are, but we have a nearly infinite number of possible goals, not just for vacations today in our lives. Life does not come to us in standard packages any more. The world has become very complex.

Think of falling in love for example. The basic values may still be there but they have obviously become more diverse. I have been divorced and remarried, and every one of my four daughters have been divorced and only one has remarried. Each of the others has developed different romantic possibilities so far.

More marriages end in divorce today than ever before, but that does not make marriage or divorces automatically good or bad. Lessons learned? Many people are waiting until later in life to get married, or are not getting married at all but have found other options with somewhat similar goals.

An interesting article appeared not all that long ago in which the writer describes all the romantic possibilities available today to anyone today. It was a diverse list and she went into great detail.

At the end of it, however, she surprisingly acknowledged that no matter what the diversity, most people today are still looking for a "soul mate". Perhaps you agree, perhaps not. In any event, our lives are obviously not as simple as the lives of Canadian geese. Where do we go with all this? The new edition of my marriage book will come out next year.

Canadian Geese still provide a model for nature's *Intentionality*, introduced in Part 1, Scene 3. Early 20th century phenomenologists claimed *Intentionality* the most basic and undeniable characteristic of consciousness. Edmund Husserl claimed in the first half of the twentieth century that consciousness is always consciousness (of), always ahead of itself. He claimed that this is an indisputable proposition, beyond any challenge from philosophy or science.

Now you begin to understand from the (of) why I mimic early phenomenologists with my dangling prepositions. That is true as far as it goes, but Husserl and other early phenomenologists as it turns out had a far too *limited* understanding of what might be called the *Field of Intentionality*.

Husserl claimed too little, not too much. Intentionality is vast, far beyond what early definitions were definitions (of).

One way to put this is that they ignored the *Bodies* out of which Intentionality emerges. Clarification of this came from the French psychologist-philosopher Maurice Merleau-Ponty, whom I studied in graduate school under Professor James Edie.

Merleau-Ponty focused on *Perception* itself as *an Active* rather than *Passive* processes, that *you Engage in the meaning of everything, even before and following Perception.*

Following C. S. Peirce without saying so, for Merleau-Ponty all of nature is intentional in its own way. Everything today called a Complex System has Intentional characteristics, including Nature itself. That does not necessarily include self-awareness as some elemental animals and plants. Hardly anything today just stands still all by itself.

Your nervous system is not just *Registering* something. *As you Perceive something through your senses, you are Shaping its meaning from the very get-go.* Tell me about your car or the car you *wish* you had. What is it? You are *Engaged* in what your car means to you.

Embodiment

Its meaning is *yours* from the first moment you saw it, as is the breakfast cereal you eat.

You are Engaged in everything from the ground up. *You live in your world. I live in mine. Grandma lives in hers. That is fascinating, but even more fascinating, we can share things with each other, which will be considered in far more detail in Part 3.*

When Merleau-Ponty's started a revolution in understanding Perception, he erased the gap between Subject and Object. That is what *dawned on me* as I sat reading him and listening to Prof. Edie.

Note: Animals know this already inherently. They just haven't stopped to think about it.

There is actually a long wiggly and curved line that runs from Peirce to Husserl to Heidegger to Merleau-Ponty, and from there all the way to Complex Systems today.

I just summarized the 20th century in Evolutionary Thinking, and this theme will come up again and again in this book. Stimulus-Response may be useful for limited purposes, but it is an *objective abstraction* from the way things actually operate.

Remember when I spoke of *Frame problems?* The classical Stimulus-Response reaction creates a Frame problem that often results in Framing Out many things that need to be included in understanding (1) what you are talking about, (2) including you yourself as who is doing the talking.

You are an Active Agent in the Active World you live in. You are not a machine; you are a work of art. Aren't you glad?

If you are a scientist who just developed or discovered a new formula or contraption, it is not just some *objective thing* but an *Active Thing* or it wouldn't be here. And it is *yours*. It is part of you, so you need to help it along, not just drop your discovery off at the delivery room, as many scientists do with their products. We will come back to this in Part 3, Scene 3.

As stated by C. S. Peirce, all nature is *Active*, not as some powerful force flowing *through* things, the mistake made by his friend William James and others. It is *not* powered by the *Vital Force* that early evolutionary theories believed. *Things themselves are active.* Peirce made that as clear as the nose on your face over a hundred years ago.

The Vital Force (élan vital) theory of Henri Bergson was very popular in some circles at first, which is understandable, given the alternatives known at the time, but it fell apart when no scientist was able to locate this force anywhere.

The secret is things themselves. There is no force driving them, they are the force of sorts in themselves, and in everything else.

In this respect, Peirce anticipated Dynamic Complex Systems, which will be considered in more detail in Scene 4. Peirce realized this before Husserl, Heidegger, or Merleau-Ponty. Dynamic Complex Systems then carries it farther with such notions as *Attractors* and *Affordances*. But I hear some of you beginning to yawn, right? So for now, let's go back to geese and humans.

Have you set any goals lately? Do you have any target dates for reaching them? How many projects do you have right now? Do you remember which ones are which? What I am saying is that all our lives are *projects*, conscious or unconscious. *Life* as Andy Clark suggests in his recent book listed in Recommended Books, is about *Surfing Uncertainty*.

This is what we and the geese do for a living. Even geese have uncertainties like weather, goose hunters, snapping turtles, whatever. If somebody drained the lake for crops where they went last year, they have to find a new place, and *the only way they really know where the new one is when they get there and it feels good. How true for all of us humans too, right?*

Where are you making your *nest* today, this week, this month, this year, next whenever? When we get there, as in the case of geese, it *feels* good to be there. *Again, we are not only pigs and chickens; we are also geese, feeling our way to somewhere.*

Life is a project of projects. Every day is a project. In many projects, we set and reach our goals not just by planning them with forethought. *We reach them by feeling our way, often without much thinking about it on the way there. Canadian geese find their way around just fine, and they do it spontaneously.*

No goose clearly defines ahead of time how to reach projects, let alone needs special education classes. The wind blows, it rains or snows, whatever. It just happens. Sometimes we humans may need special education classes, but in the end we still have to learn through Experience, which is how Evolution learns. That is how we as humans learn most of the time. More about that in Scenes 5 and 6.

Experience and Feeling is very understated and rated. They provide a deeper and broader context for virtually everything we do. Right now you are reading this book. What was your goal when you started reading it? Are you still progressing toward that goal? Is this project really worth it? Whatever the answer to any of those questions, you are *feeling* your way along.

Who is it who said that we find out where we are going by going there? Doesn't that fit most of what we do in proceeding with our goals? Even if you knew why you picked up this book, is the goal you had in mind the same one you have now?

My goal in writing this Scene was rather general when I first started. My goals shaped and reshaped themselves several times during the writing, as every draft has shaped and reshaped itself since.

That happens to geese, too, although not as often perhaps as with us. If they discover that the lake where they usually land is full of snapping turtles or men with guns, they change their course and try to find one without snapping turtles or men with guns. Ever had that kind of Experience?

Evolution itself is given to solving problems. This is why it gets up in the morning, just as *you* do, if only to reach for the alarm clock to shut it off. *Supra-Instinctive Coping Strategies* will unfold in the coming Scenes. They are Nature's way of doing things.

I am slowly shifting "What *comes* to us" to "What *dawns* on us". What *dawns* on me is that no matter how long plans take, the mother of invention is involved in everything we do, if we allow that. The mother of invention may not concern finding a new mate but how to find new ways to treat that mate. As stated earlier, what "comes to us is creative, not a temptation to commit *destructive* things.

The emphasis here and now is on how often *What Dawns on You* is not just a *memory* retrieved from internal computers. Instead, something *dawns* on us, as it does when Joe Black realizes that the hospital is not a good visiting place for him, or in an even more interesting way, when Bond and Madeleine have just survived the attack of the brute, suddenly something *Dawns on them* that they have not done before.

In case you are wondering, it is easy to distinguish "dawning" from "temptation". The difference is radical, especially in time. Dawn-in passes the test of time. Temptation usually flunks big-time. Dawning is creative, temptation is inherently frustrating. Dawning helps you "feel your oats" (as they say where I come from), but temptation frustrates you with never getting enough whatever when you do. Dawning inspires, temptation tickles and then depresses.

As we proceed, it is interesting how surviving a crisis can precipitate doing things in a different way. We will continue that theme through the rest of this book. Man's extremity is God's opportunity, but not only God's, as Bond and Madeleine demonstrate.

Embodiment

When something *dawns* it is often in stages. First the light begins to show and then the sun breaks through and the light shines. See why I have gradually moved without thinking about it from the phrase *what comes to us* to *what dawns on us*?

Situations are often complex. Given his traditional killer instincts, what *dawns* on Bond as he stands over his wounded but arch-villain foster-brother Oberhauser with gun in hand? Bond empties his cartridge on the ground instead of shooting him.

Perhaps the movie's ending is better than the one I will suggest, but I can't help putting myself in Bond's shoes and wondering what I would do.

Oberhauser's life seems like the very Embodiment of the Biblical story of Cain who killed his brother Abel, who was more loved by his father than he was. Oberhauser has outdone Cain far more than "one better". Before killing Bond his foster-brother, he is also insanely jealous, and not only kills his own father, all of Bond's lovers in all Bond movies, and M, his mother surrogate, he now plans to destroy Bond's livelihood and lobotomize Bond while Madeleine watches, and then kill her.

This is even worse that today's Radicals who are only successful in destroying things. He leaves Cain in the shade with no lemonade. Would you agree?

You may perhaps start thinking what you would do if you were in Bond's shoes. I acknowledge that this is one of those few places where it is difficult to say whether you would like my idea.

I personally would have shot him. After all, he is asking me to do that, *although* if I stopped to think that Bonnie, like Madeleine, is watching, wanting me to give up my job of killing bad people, I'd still kill him as he asked, *then* throw away my gun, *then* resign my job as I passed the new M.

I don't know Madeline but I do know Bonnie. I'd go over and on my knees beg Bonnie to forgive me. She would forgive me, agreeing it was not really a *killing* but an *Agent-Assisted Suicide*.

Besides, she would realize, given his evil genius, he would escape incarceration, requiring another life threatening story, and Bonnie would love cancelling that possibility.

So I promise Bonnie I would slit my wrist on the nearest piece of glass rather than do that. Besides, a 007 agent has a great retirement package. Besides, she'd divorce me if I ever killed anybody else, and she knows I don't want that, etc. So we would have driven off into the sunset in our old Corvette. Better ending, right?

Probably not, but does it make me a bad person if I kill the very Epitome of Evil? As I imagined doing it, I really felt good, and it would be the first *Agent Assisted Suicide* in the history of the double O series, right? So give me a break, OK?

If you have a better ending if it were you instead of Bond or me, please send it to me.

While you are at it, you might find a better ending too for *Meet Joe Black*. After such and intricate and complex development, I agree with some critics that the ending is rather corny and contrived, even if it is sweet. So send that one to me, too.

PART 2
SCENE 4 UTILIZING OPTIONS

Bats have an incredible ability to pick out mosquitos in the dark with their bodily senses far beyond anything we humans possess. As you learned in Part 1, bats have ears with which we cannot compete. We do not have sonar. Nor do we have hairs on our skin as sensitive as theirs. All ours can do is stand on end while watching horror movies. Bats are sensitive to everything around them. We are not, but we could be far more sensitive than we are, and develop a better traffic record, etc.

If we could see, listen, and feel the way a bat does, our senses would tell us not just what is happening now but what will happen next. That is how a bat operates with mosquitos. It is not a matter of abstract calculation; it is a matter of *sensitivity*, which is forever minding the future. It is like when we sense what the person is trying to say or will say next. Ever helped someone say something they are trying to say?

One point of this Scene is that we humans don't usually use all the senses we already have. When you are talking with someone, for example, it is good to pay attention not just to *what* is said but *how* it is said, the facial expression, tone and volume of the voice, the feelings being expressed in gestures and movement, including what is likely to be said next. The bats would be proud of you if you do that.

As a human you learn to pay attention to *clues and cues*. You are not just talking *to* someone; you are talking *with* someone, or are you? It is often important to notice when speaking with someone whether they appear sad, tense, anxious, angry, frustrated, or whatever. Bats have no ability to do that, except perhaps with other bats.

Conversation can easily become a fine art, beginning with such practices as guessing what is going on with whom you are conversing, by beginning sentences with: "You look (or sound) like…" or "You seem to feel….." and if possible, name a feeling, not a thought or idea. Again, it is not as if you have to play therapist, but it may draw the person into the conversation rather than back away. We will come back to that in Part 3, Scene 4.

Bats usually have only one chance at their targets, and you may have several. If you are working your way up to asking somebody to marry you or take the job, car, loan, or whatever you are seeking, even simple observing of emotional cues and clues can be important.

If you are shaking someone's hand in a crowd and their hand feels cold or clammy, you shouldn't usually comment on how anxious the person seems to be, or you make them feel even more anxious, but you might want to reach out and shake the person's hand warmly with both your hands, and/or assure the person that you are a friend. Smiling can also help, etc.

Once you start doing this kind of thing, it will come to you spontaneously in time what to do next. You will get the hang of it. Nobody paints a masterpiece in the first painting. If you still need help in Part 3, Scene 4, come back here for a refresher course about basics. *It is far too easy to become preoccupied with what is wrong with the other person and lose track of who they are* and/or *need in the process.*

Bats not only utilize all their senses, they seek *new options* in all directions, which is a special kind of sensitivity. Bats remind me of Nassim Taleb, whose *The Black Swan* I have mentioned before. Once upon a time "black swan" was a phrase to describe a nonexistent creature that only existed in fairy tales. Then they were discovered in Australia.

Taleb generalizes such discoveries as *Black Swans events*, symbolizing that what was once thought "impossible" could create great new possibilities. He develops this farther in *Antifragile: Things that Gain from Disorder*. It is nearly 500 pages long, but any few pages at a time are great daily "devotional" reads. They suggest new possibilities in all directions, even if you thought them impossible before you read him.

Antifragile is not a word in the dictionary, so don't bother to look, but just putting a hyphen between "anti" and "fragile" gives you the idea. You don't want to be Fragile (losing your grip) in an Antifragile (chaotic) world.

In other words, he describes how live in a world filled with *Black Swan* events and remain focused on something, whatever it is, without getting disoriented and dysfunctional, missing in the process new possibilities that Black Swans provide. It takes acute sensitivity, and *thinking outside the box (or package)*.

He, like Damasio, leaves me in the shade in his ability to draw together diverse fields of thought into everyday life and make them *inspiring*. Illustration: His "Fat Tony and Socrates" passages gave me ideas that led to my own similar but rather different comments about Socrates.

So he does not mean for you to imitate him, but inspire you to take a different but perhaps similar direction in your own way. You wouldn't want to be dysfunctional in a chaotic world, would you?

Taleb started professionally on Wall Street, where three of my grandchildren now work. He talks about his specialty there but does not mean to train you in that field. He means simply to help you take off your shackles (packages) and do something different.

On Wall Street he specialized in the confusing world of *Stock Options*, which bothers him no more than it does a bat when it finds itself in a field of a thousand mosquitos.

Bats are always aware of what is happening not only in front of them but to the side, and even behind them, and can move spontaneously. *Like a bat, Taleb plays his Options quickly and wisely.*

He is a graduate of the famous Wharton School of Business, but what he learned on Wall Street was through Experience. Skill in Stock Options require a very different perspective from looking ahead very rationally for long-range goals.

As I understand options, thanks mostly to my grandson Ben, you purchase at a relatively small cost an "option" to buy the stock *if* at a given date it reaches a certain price, not knowing for sure meanwhile what the rest of the market will do. There are *call* options to buy and *put* options to sell.

The interesting part here to me is that the price is intrinsically linked to the price of *everything around it*, which is what makes me think again of bats. It requires great sensitivity to the option's surroundings where *everything else* is going on, not just the particular option. It is like a bat in a wide field of mosquitos making a decision which mosquito to focus on, realizing that the mosquitos around it may be moving quickly in different directions.

Watching pro basketball games is for me a similar mental exercise. It could be soccer, I suppose, but not for a Hoosier like me. Team members are continually interrelating with each other in a fast moving game. In basketball, everything is chaotic and the possibilities are endless, but Black Swan Options requiring relatively low investment can provide big reward possibilities.

A guard brings the ball down the floor and there are all kinds of Black Swan Options, forward, to the sides, and even behind. This requires instant sensitivity of where every player, friend or foe, *is* and *will be* in the next few moments. To me it resembles Life for a bat.

I am surprised that there are no professional teams named the Bats. If there are bats in the rafters of the giant gyms where basketball games occur and they could talk, bats would tell you Steph Curry has long been one of their favorite players. They might even claim that they taught him everything he knows.

I stopped to watch the boy next door "shoot hoops" on the basket beside the driveway. He apologized about his missed shots. I said not to be discouraged, that after a few hundred practice shots, he would get the hang of it big time. I said that I hadn't picked up a basketball for a very long time myself.

So he tossed the ball to me at about the three point range. It was first surprising to me how heavy the basketball was. However, I thought it would be like bicycle riding, something you never forget, so I tried to adjust for the weight problem, and let the shot go. It was more or less on the mark, but fell two or three feet short. I shrugged and told him I obviously needed some practice.

Back to Bond, when he is in a fight like the one on the train he demonstrates long Experience *and* great Sensitivity when he sees close to the open train door a row of heavy barrels linked with the rope at the end, which he then uses when he goes from behind the brute strangling Madeleine. He couldn't throw the brute out the nearby train door without help, so the barrels helped. How many of us would have noticed those interconnected barrels?

The wisdom that comes from Experience also makes me think of my father, who had only a high school education and worked in a company with lots of people with Ph.D. credentials, most of whom who he considered inept at simple things like pulling into the Lilly entrance without causing an accident. He read the Britannica Encyclopedia to educate himself, and learned the rest from Experience.

Isn't it strange that university enrollments are dropping for the first time, while community college enrollments are rising? I am not opposed to university education, where I have worked for many years, but aren't there lessons here for universities today?

For the first time, many university graduates are now failing to get jobs in fields for which they are supposedly qualified, are living with mom and dad, and/or have to take lesser paying jobs in lesser fields than those for which they were supposedly prepared. To make matters worse, how can they pay back huge educational loans?

Today we face *fragile* situations. But there is a folk expression among farmers where I grew up: "There is more than one way to skin a cat" (meaning very big cats of course). No matter how big and threatening the problems may be that face us, surprisingly new *options* may open to us if we keep our senses awake.

Utilize your sense of your surroundings like a bat does, right? Now I will shut up about bats. I promise, more or less.

PART 2
SCENE 5 THE DYNAMICS OF TINKERING

This Scene matches Scene 5 in Part 1, blending Trial and Error into *Tinkering*, where the only problem is that it can become endless. Momma Bear and I Tinker, but for me that came to a sudden end. With Momma Raccoon it continued for years.

Although Dynamic Complex Systems do not always start with a clearly definable beginning, they become more complex as they develop, and end with all the problems solved. The whole process is Dynamic, which becomes obvious even in the relatively brief period when Jesse and Momma Bear relate to each other.

Every time you bracket or frame something, you may be leaving something out that needs more attention, which in time becomes obvious. At the same time, however, you may know some things definitely work, but you don't know exactly why. It just does. Complex Systems and Nature often work that way.

So when you change *something*, it may at the same time change *nothing*, *everything*, and/or *some particular* thing(s) in fascinating and perhaps confusing ways. *Tinkering is working with desired Effects with or without necessarily understanding Causes.*

We therefore need Tinkering as long as we don't have the Effects we want. Causes are a side issue. Theories work or don't the same way Frames do or don't. The crucial issue is the Effects, not the Causes. It's Nature's way of doing things.

Theories come and go, even what appear to be successful theories, except in pure math and "truths" *within* given frames, but even those in complex processes may leave out things that later affect what is inside the frame. Evolution may appear to stop its tinkering momentarily, but not for long. "There is always something", as Roseannadanna says.

Evolution always faces chaos trying to swallow it up. That is Life folks; get used to it. A big question facing us every moment is, what do we Tinker with? It could be anything, but it isn't, as Experience will teach us.

Tinkering is involved in whatever we face ahead of us that seems unfinished, which is different for every one of us individually and socially. Time is always passing us going in the other direction, and we are not just going south for winter vacations.

Our possibilities are far wider than for most animals. We and our surroundings are constantly changing in bigger ways. What is it for us at any moment? I can't answer that question for me any better than you can for you. We are forever Tinkering whether we like it or not.

Tinkering is often unconscious, but sometimes it becomes very conscious. You have an itch, you know it and you scratch it, but you often scratch an itch without even knowing it. Do you think everybody scratching an itch notices it consciously? Watch and see.

Sometimes itches or whatever come and go quickly. Other times things preoccupy us and require a lot of time, like writing a book, buying a computer or a car, getting a job, getting married, raising a kid, etc.

There are always big and/or small Unfinished Configurations (*Gestalts*). A Gestalt by definition is not Static but Alive. Ask any Gestalt Therapist.

Consciously or unconsciously you develop a HHHypothesis, Experiment with it, Test the Results, and Tinker until *Something Works* and then Tinker some more to make work even better. This method was not invented by Science or Rationality. Nature does it all the time.

With you and me personally, our Tinkering needs differ from those of anyone else in the billions of humans who now live on the earth. For humans this may require some Reflective Thought, but even that has to be tested by Experience. That's Life.

Life is always changing. What appeared to work earlier does not necessarily work as well today, just as the Penicillin my dad helped develop doesn't work today as well as antibiotics that have replaced it.

Only completely Framed problem are solved forever. 2+2 will always equal 4 in a calculator, but Open Systems are always alive and kicking as long as they are alive. Consider you and me. We are only Framed problems when we are dead.

If something is not working, either improve it or find something else that *does*, at least for now. Life is as simple as that. Nature and our animal friends invented Tinkering long before we ever appeared on earth. Call it a gift of God or whatever.

James Bond has amazing *Tools* available. That incredibly expensive car that he leaves at the bottom of a river is no Model T Ford, nor is the one you drive to the grocery store. If Henry Ford were alive today, he would be impressed. He would also be impressed with how many hit and run criminals were killing pedestrians today in LA, leaving the bodies they crushed on the street. Now we're back to rooster types of humans. They would be perfect candidates lately to burn down federal courthouses.

The focus here is on what can we do when things are not working. The only way to solve such problems is to learn from earlier experience and do things differently than we did before, see what happens, then Tinker with it and get it as nearly right as we can for the time being. That is always the history of our country.

Life has a very long history. Rationality is one of its children. There may of course be probabilities, but there's always something else.

There are two different ways to deal with human *Coping Problems*: (1) The rational/reflective way. *Try consciously* and reflectively to *design* something new as a plan, then *do* it, and see if it *Works*. or (2) The emotional/spontaneous way. *Allow something to Emerge*, what will in time "Dawn on You" as a solution and follow what in your Experience *Works*.

They both can *Work*, either alone or blended together, depending on the kind of problem involved end what kind of person you are. Most of us are both (1) and (2) above, whether we are aware of it or not. It happens all the time.

New Subject: A new way to integrate Reason and Emotion has occurred in the field of Risk Assessment. It began when the established psychological researcher in risk assessment Paul Slovic, whom I mentioned earlier, was crossing the street by foot one day in heavy fast moving traffic and realized that *risks are emotional, not just statistical events*. Haven't you ever crossed a street on foot in heavy traffic? If not, you haven't really lived. Overstatement, right? Not really!

Slovic had been running very complex research in Risk Management when he realized how statistics often fail to realize how important *Emotions* are in those risks, which should not be ignored even statistically. *Strange as it may seem, past Risk Assessment usually Ignored Emotional Issues. Slovic's* recent work has made enormous differences in assessing and treating such diverse issues as advertising, medicine, and genocide (sound familiar? If not it will in Part 3).

It is all too easy to get lost, for example, in statistical data and neglect emotional components involved. To Stalin one death may be a tragedy, but a million is a statistic. *Numbers and Nerves* is the short book co-authored by Slovic and his son Scott. I became briefly acquainted with Scott, who agreed to present a Skype paper at the Hawaii symposium I mentioned earlier.

Embodiment

In his other books, Paul Slovic makes major use of Damasio's book on Descartes, especially his focus on *Somatic Markers*, but let's go a little deeper than Slovic into the nature of *Nerves and Numbers*.

Our neurons are not only found in enormous numbers; they are *Living Numbers*. They function in ways very different from the numbers you learned in school. *Neurons are not simply Objects, they are Active and Self-Organizing Agents that have no meaning apart from their Life together*.

That is very different from Numbers found on computer screens. Neurons are *Alive* in ways numbers on blackboards or computer screens are *not*.

Neurons cannot be easily added or subtracted, multiplied or divided without missing something in Life. Life operates in Dynamic and Complex ways. *So complexity is not limited to the frontal lobes, nor are those lobes the location of the mind anyway*. Have you ever wondered where exactly in the skull consciousness is located? Let me know if you do. We might both win a Nobel Award.

The mind resembles an Integrated Circuit. It is nowhere in particular. It is everywhere in your body.

Numbers on computer screens are meaningful of course, but they are abstractions of living numbers. They are meaningful as *Tools* we utilize, like a hammer or saw. They may be intricately useful, but it takes *Embodiment* to bring them to Life. Disembodied research can easily become as destructive as fictitiously in Oberhauser, or historically as in Hitler or Stalin.

Paul Slovic does not put it exactly this way, but thanks to books like *Numbers and Nerves*, we are beginning to understand on a popular level that Numbers Without Nerves are lacking. That is why I say numbers without nerves are *Disembodied*.

Some Artificial Intelligence (AI) experts are beginning to realize that computers do not resemble human thinking processes as easily as they thought, and they are also realizing they have a *very* long way to go to make computers human.

Computers usually proceed by way of *Frames*. That is not the way either Nature or Consciousness proceed. Nature never read a book on logic. It proceeds as the mind usually does, spontaneously and without that "benefit". That is why experts are working now on developing computers that can learn as humans do, but again they have a *very* long way to go.

As I said earlier, a Tool is an extension of its user, as the philosopher Martin Heidegger said long ago. A hammer can *be* lots of things, depending on the human who has it in hand. A hammer by itself is meaningless.

Numbers properly used, as the Slovics demonstrate, can become what *real* numbers, *living numbers*, are as they become *Embodied* with emotional resources beyond their *Disembodied* meaning. Disembodied numbers, like other tools, can just as easily kill someone as save them. Ask Oberhauser. He was very high tech, right?

The same can be said of Rationality. Rationality is a tool for undistending things objectively and rationally, but it has possible flaws, as shown in Taleb's imagined dialogue between Socrates and Fat Tony. Socrates just doesn't "get it" when Taleb's Tony tries to explain the primacy of Experience. No wonder the Slovics insisted on getting numbers and nerves together. They need each other.

I love my computer as much as you do. It is part of me the same way Heidegger describes hammers. Every tool in my life is part of me, including Rationality. They have no real Life within them.

Nerves not only invented huge numbers, they invented the very complex rationalities Nature employs without ever stopping to think about it. Rationality at its best as stated earlier copies Nature.

Look at how Momma Bear solved her problems with her special child. Use her as a model and solve one of your problems, and she will be proud of you, right?.

Now I will sit down and shut up.

PART 2
SCENE 6 FROM NOVICE TO EXPERT

This Scene focuses on the dynamics of the learning process not as what you traditionally learn in public school, taking tests on what the teacher told you to *remember*. Here your learning is from *Direct Experience and Practice*.

Experience does not illustrate theory; theory illustrates Experience. You have to begin with Experience to really understand things. That is why experience, even Stories built on Experience, can often teach more than abstract rules and outlines.

Fortunately, my most worthwhile learning in school began with Oral Hildebrand and his Experiential way of teaching math. Classes like that beat classes in Indoctrination any day of the week.

Dreyfus divides *Coping Skills* into 5 different stages. As described earlier, each stage describes a different level of skill development, and each requires *Learning from Experience*. Distinctions in the frontal lobes of the brain lean more toward emotion, experience, and the arts in one hemisphere and in the other, rationality, calculation, and math, although Dreyfus speaks more philosophically than neurologically.

He uses examples like learning how to drive a car or play chess. My experience with farmers, music, basketball, and in math from Oral Hildebrand are similar. As I say elsewhere, he forced me to learn for myself the basic theorems of geometry. You may or may not had similar personal learning experiences yourself. Or have you?

Learning from Experience takes time, in school or out. Ultimately, it concerns how to cope with Life. In Coping Skills, Experience, not Rote Learning, are the most basic methods needed, not the other way around. What is learned in rote learning is in itself useless.

Embodiment

The final level, Expertise, requires lots and lots of practice during which some things may wane rather than wax. Expert athletes begin to lose their edge in their thirties, but as my voice coach in college told me, although tenors lose their voices in their sixties, basses like me can sing forever, which is why I told the college basketball coach I'd rather sing.

You can see perhaps where I am going with this. Whatever the process, Evolution rarely leaves anything where it started, for good or ill. Despite what my voice coach told me in college, I won't be singing oratorios on my death bed, and I may be losing my mental marbles by then, too. But let's go back to the good stuff, how Coping Skills develop to their max.

Dreyfus is not the only writer to describe Coping Skills. What is unique to his version is his focus on *Experiential Learning*, which is *Bottom-Up* so to speak.

Stage 1 is Novice, which for most of us begins in early life and our parents, something that will be developed concerning ethics much later in this book.

My dad and mom went to Westland School, an even smaller school than in *Hoosiers* that won the state championship, but years before that my dad's team got as far as the Regional level.

You can imagine why he was so excited to have Roll in the final game. I was very young, but we actually heard the *real* game on the radio.

I was only about 8 years old and remember nothing about the game itself except that Roll won, as I recall 32-28. What I remember most is my dad's excitement, exclaiming that they did it, as his team did, with "ball control".

I did not even know what that meant at the time, but his lesson sank deeper into me since then I realized that the players in his and

Roll's tiny country schools had been playing together since they were probably 5 years old and had lots of Experience together not just alone but together in ball control.

Their extensive Practice together had grown to a level where they were more far more skilled in "ball control" than their huge urban (and always changing) high-schools.

What was important here in this book is how much time is usually needed to move through the stages of Coping Skills, *and how socially oriented it can be*, which Dreyfus gives little attention.

It took many years for what my father said to completely soak in concerning teams. At Lilly he had 50 people as I recall working for him in the *production* of Penicillin.

Team-Mate Experience makes basketball more interesting than chess to me. You may have had team-mate experiences that are similar. You may also recall that Raccoons usually work as a team.

The basic point here is the Novice stage grows quite naturally through the other stages that Dreyfus describes. The Stages are part of Evolution's many lessons for us all, no matter what stages we represent at the moment. *But learning is not just an individual process, despite what teachers often assume.*

More concerning parental learning will be described in Ethical Development in Part 4, Scene 2. For now, let's consider for a few moments how we learn things socially as we move from family into the social world. then we will come back to the stages themselves.

How did it "dawn on me" to start each of the Parts of this book with a Movie? A movie is a *story, which begins for most of us very early in Life.*

Let's consider movies as stories that take another step from mom and dad, telling stories to you right in the midst of your Senses. You are actually Living there in a movie.

Movies move us. We have already dealt with movies as *Empathetic*. Here the emphasis is *how* they *Affect/Effect* us. *Affect/Effects* concern Feelings; *Effect* concerns *Doing* something differently, embodying our *Supra-Instinctive Strategies*, so to speak.

Adult Movies at their best are Children's Stories for Grown-Ups. We do not go to movies for "lessons" on how to behave. We are thrown directly into concrete situations where we are "exposed" in "circumstances" that encourage us to Make Sense of them.

How do Movies Move us? Good movies are not just entertainment, they move us not by "lessons" but by concrete exposure to dilemmas where we feel and identify with characters in such a way that we learn directly with them. We *gather Experientially* whatever "lessons" *we* formulate through the movie.

It is difficult to walk out of movies like *Tears of the Sun* (or more recently *Sicario*) without dramatic changes in our feelings, attitudes, *and* behavior. Other movies like *Meet Joe Black* approach us more gently, but there too it is difficult to walk out the same way we walked in.

What this is leading up to is that movies can be experienced not just as "entertainment" but in terms of their Affect/Effects.

Now we can we can return to the coping skill stages again and move from Novice and Advanced Beginner to Competency to Proficiency.

Competence involves ability during experiences to assess situations in order to focus on what represents what Dreyfus calls the ability to shift from what he calls "left brain analytic" to "right brain holistic" in solving situational problems.

Back to my experience in basketball. On my failures in junior high-school with basketball, I turned to my more successful record in music, my studies, and working to save money for college, where I was one day playing intramural basketball at our small liberal arts college one day and at 6'4" I discovered that I could dunk the basketball, which nobody on our small college team could do.

Our college coach, who was watching for new prospects, called me over to the side and said he had a place for me on his team traveling to the Orient this summer. I said I am sorry but was too busy with my studies and music as my extracurricular work. He stared at me a if I were some combination of stupid and insane.

He just said: "Music?" I said Yes, that I would be singing the role of Figaro in Mozart's the "Marriage of Figaro" with an imported violin section from New York and would be traveling to Japan this summer s a soloist, thinking that might impress him. He just said again "Music?" He turned, walked away, disgusted with me, and never spoke to me again.

But you can't do everything, right? More about music in Part 3, Scene 1.

Stage 4 is *Proficiency*. Dreyfus' case here is Contextual, Complex, and even Unconscious because things are done without Reflective Thinking at all. *Dreyfus calls for learning directly first from Experience, Not afterward.*

He uses illustrations from driving and chess. In both cases you are sensitive by Experience to know what to do next that may require changing immediately what you have been learning without even thinking about it.

He illustrates with the driver who drives not by consciously considering different options and situations or even strategies, but making spontaneous changes that are needed in concrete experience, that no amount of reflective teaching can teach. His colorful illustration is what he calls *driving by the seat of your pants*.

Stage 5 is Expert. Dreyfus describes this as a single field of vision or whatever that requires different kinds of strategies and quick decisions in different kinds of situations all at once, i.e., a Vast Repertoire of Experience in diverse situations gathers itself together into a single action.

One of Dreyfus' illustrations of expert is a chess master's ability to embody more than 50,000 positions and in tournaments make the next move in 5-10 seconds. This is indeed impressive.

Granting that the coping strategies in chess are far beyond basketball, basketball is nevertheless interesting. In basketball the moves are nearly 5-10 seconds faster than in chess, and involve 9 other players on the court moving at the same time, 4 of which are on your team, OK? Basketball is a much more complex environment than a chess board to me. But I am a Hoosier, right?

Dreyfus doesn't get deeply into neurobiology in his work as a Heidegger-style phenomenologist, and although he does not mention Peirce nor his friend William James, he does mention another early Pragmatist, John Dewey, who called for the "thoughtless mastery of the everyday", which for Dreyfus suggests Expertise.

Since Expertise is where you know what to do spontaneously in *extremely* complex situations without stopping to think about it, I he might consider at least a few Mothers as Experts. Does a mother know what to do to care for her child, especially a "special" child? She learns from the inherent experience of mothers before her and since then in her own experience, so she is on her road to Expertise. Ask my wife Bonnie how she raised her own special child Dominique for years before we met.

And of course there is Momma Raccoon who deserves at least proficiency, right? In case you recall my mom's problems concerning pigs, we parents all have our faults. She was otherwise a great mom, a great mediator between my dad and me, and I definitely owe my artistic orientation to her, not my dad.

You probably have parental stories of your own, right? All in all, I had problems with both parents, but they survived having to deal with me, and I survived my parents. How about you?

PART 2
SCENE 7 HUMAN CULTURE

Part 2 has continued similar themes from Part 1, but has moved the focus from animals to humans, with input from animals as described in Part 1. In Scene 7, that focus will turn from individual to social or collective issues, as did Part 1, Scene 7 concerning honeybee society.

Except for Bill's board of directors and the party at the end in *Meet Joe Black*, there is little *Collectivity* of the sort present in a Honeybee Hive. It is about both individual and family relationships. Nor is there much *Collectivity* in *Spectre*, which has a huge collaborative setting, but the focus is again mostly on individual and family relationships, not on a vast society, *unless* maniacs go berserk. Even the collaborations of Bond, M, Q, and Moneypenny are mostly family affairs.

The primary focus in *Spectre* is on Bond's relation to Madeleine, set in the context of his relation to his missing family of origin, and hers too when we meet her father Mr. White, who dies not far into the movie and far away from her. Nevertheless we are moving in the *direction* of broad social issues in countering Oberhauser's attempts to rule the whole world, including the use of genocidal strategies, which is why Mr. White left Oberhauser's organization. More on Genocide in Part 3.

There are many resemblances between how Neurons behave individually and how they behave as parts of a whole by way of neuron populations, just as the neurological progression of Parts 1 and 2 move toward the broad cultural embodiments of Parts 3 and 4.

The best descriptions of neurological processes in relation to our social environment are found in the two short books by Walter Freeman and the much longer books of Antonio Damasio and Andy Clark listed in Recommended Books *if* you want to reach into the depths of the collective pig-wallow where we all live.

For me the clearest model for culture is to begin with (1) each neuron within us as a tree, with each having a stem, body, and dendrite branches linked to billions of other tiny trees, (2) creating within us as individuals a collective bodily tree of trees, which in turn reaches out to (3) other humans within (4) our culture as a collective cultural tree of trees of trees in which we all participate together.

You may have to re-read this sentence a time or two to let it soak in, but the whole thing is our *Embodied Complex System* within another and then another, etc. *It is a huge family affair.*

Freeman describes the basic character of evolutionary change as Unification, Wholeness, and Intentionality. That resembles Peirce's evolutionary model: Union, Difference, and Creativity. It also resembles the Gestalt therapy model is *The Youniverse: the Spirit of the 21st Century 2020*: Wholeness, Dialogue, and Intentionality.

One easy way to describe in few words the Neurological Complexity of collective behavior is with a honeybee story that was not included in this Scene in Part 1. Although the neurological system of bees has relatively few neurons compared to our billions, they show remarkable resemblances to us. While my life with pigs lasted only a few moments, in contrast to 3 years with raccoons, my life as part of bee society lasted nearly 10 years.

The unanswered question in my mind for a long time was how do honeybees communicate with each other? How do they "decide" things? *Why* for example is it the old queen who leaves so the new "queen in waiting" can leave the hive she has so faithfully maintained for so long? And how do the bees "decide" which bees would stay or leave, swarming around the queen as they leave? Was it just more "experienced" bees who leave? And why do bees rarely sting when they are swarming? How do they "decide" these things?

A lot of it is a matter of Learning from their Experience what Works. It may have accidentally worked once and when they noticed the same thing several times and made it into an ongoing habit.

Consider that I had noticed that when a big bundle of bees left the hive with the old queen to find a new hive for her, they first land for a while on a nearby branch, I suppose they had learned from experience to give their scouts time to find a new hive location.

Whatever their reason, I found it easy to cut off the limb where they landed and carry the big bundle of bees to the new but hitherto closed hive I had ready for a new swarm of bees.

Somehow they accepted me into their usual procedure. The first time I was a little nervous. But the second time was a piece of cake. *That made it possible for me to consider myself as a member of the hive. It was like being accepted by the pigs in the pig-wallow.* I was one of the "organs" in their Honeybee Embodiment. I was part of the mind of the hive, so to speak.

So that makes me not only a pig of sorts, but a "busy little bee", too. I am certainly going to pitch "our" cause when I meet with the city fathers about the seven acre extended-care housing project on the back side of my half-acre Jungle.

Anyway, I feel at least as much as my liver does about me that I was part of my honeybee hive's embodiment. As a hive we manage to function as a single body without talking with each other about it. It just worked and we noticed that. We were more than "just friends".

I have two species of lizards in my jungle. One is especially adept at "head nodding" up and down. Theories claim it is for attention, claiming their territory, or whatever. Whatever it is, it works. So I nod back, and at times they seem to notice, but that doesn't necessarily make me part of their Embodiment the way I felt I was with the bees.

However, there is another interesting bee *embodied communication* story concerning honeybees, which I've witnessed many times. In this case some of their Language is actually decipherable.

On their landing boards, some bees, instead of simply coming and going, seemed to stop to greet each other. Have they gotten drunk on honey and are celebrating on the landing board as their bar? Are they sharing stories about the big party they had last night when all the bees were in the hive? What are they doing? After watching them do this several times, and finding no better answer than the dopey ones you just read, I turned to my literary sources on honeybees.

Perhaps you already know this. In those days it was real news. Today it may be all some know about honeybees.

Authorities on bees usually refer to what they are doing as "dancing" because of the regular patterns they are tracing. A bee with a message doesn't just pick up its little cell phone and call from the pollen source, or when it gets back to the hive open its little mouth and talk about it, it *dances* its story.

The incoming bees are signaling to other bees the direction and distance to new pollen sources, so it is their way of "demonstrating" information concerning a new Attractor that can become a new Affordance for other bees.

So why don't they communicate this way about other things? Only likely answer I can imagine is that this is the only time when they are communicating specific *time and space* answers. Decent guess? Perhaps this answers that question, but how about other communication processes? Sharing Somatic Markers somehow? Playing follow the leader?

I don't know where bee dancing takes you, but it takes me back to my grad school studies in primal cultures, where music, drumming, and dancing in primal tribes and their standard ritual practices. Primals were imitating the behavior of birds and animals, but I hadn't thought of *insects*, let alone conversations among neurons. But to me, *they all fit*. How much sharing and communication is involved in a dance anywhere? More of that in Parts 3 and 4.

Of course we and animals do interact. Only today I saw a photo of a black Great Dane like the one I used to have, lying on a cot beside his owner doing yoga with him. Rafe and I never did yoga together, but when he died he had to be buried, and since he was big even for a Dane, it required my digging all day and into the night a life-sized grave. This is my only dog story in the book.

Well into a moonless night Bonnie's son Lance and his friend Skip helped me bury him, which required carrying him some distance late at night from the house to his grave. When we got there I was carrying Rafe's front feet and Skip was carrying his back feet. Lance was carrying the flashlight.

When we started to lower Rafe into the grave, his back feet slipped out of Skip's hands and that jerked his front feet out of mine. Rafe fell to the bottom of the grave, and barked an exceptionally loud WOOOOF. Skip screamed an exceptionally loud EEEEK and ran for his life.

Of course scientific types will claim that what happened to Rafe was simply that when he hit the bottom of the grave his collapsing lungs inevitably created the WOOOOF.

Perhaps that explains it scientifically. But even if it does, does that mean Rafe's "speech" was meaningless? Makes sense to me that it was his way of saying Goodbye. What do you think? In any case I swear it is a true animal story. Ask Lance. Skip, wherever he is, probably doesn't want to talk about it.

As for me, I appeal to an old folk heuristic where I come from what "dawns on me": *Every dog has his day.* (Rafe told me to add this.)

Rafe and I did do dances of sorts while playing and wrestling together, but that is as close as I can come to the movie *Dances with Wolves*. In Native American language, you could call me Dances with Dogs. (The hero gets his tribal name by being seen "dancing" with the wolf who visited his isolated military-post often while the

Indians watched from nearby.) If and when you see their dance in the movie, it is not obvious who is imitating whom, just as when Rafe danced with me. Perhaps you as a reader may have done this yourself.

Dancing however not only an art is, it is communication, no matter how non-verbal it may be. "Actions speak louder than words." My grandma told me this. *So perhaps honeybees are celebrating as well as providing information about the location of new pollen sites?*

It raises questions about our own dancing. (1) do we dance in imitation of our animal friends, (2) do we intuitively imitate our own neurological systems, or (3) is it both?

After all, our neurological systems are "dancing" in a more or less synchronized balancing act all the time. Besides that, of course, we imitate each other. Ever been dancing together in a big group of dancers? I may be getting a little carried away here, so I will simply say that my dancing neurons told me to say this.

Damasio describes beautifully with a precision beyond mine how signals move from Visceral, Tactile, Organic, and Chemical origins into new transitions with *Somatic Markers, motivated perhaps by original attractors and affordances.* This "dancing" transits up (in feed-forward, lateral, and feed-back patterns) through the Neuropil and its populations in the pre-frontal cortex and toward the grey matter.

More of this in Part 3, Scenes 1 and 5. *The point here is that dancing is universal in primal society as a way of both communicating and consolidating a tribe.* For me personally during grad school it led me eventually to the Dionysius in 69 and Fillmore East in New York City.

My point here is that dancing describes not only an important social behavior, but dancing, as with the bees, is loaded with information and broadcasts spontaneously and nonverbally wherever it is.

Embodiment

This is leading to Part 3, but first comes a movie with no dancing at all until the very end. Can you wait that out? "Don't give me that look," as my elders often told me. OK, let's move on.

PART 3

THE DAWNING OF EMBODIED CULTURE
TEARS OF THE SUN

The basic theme in Part 3 is *Embodied Cultural Values*, meaning social values rooted in Experience, not top-down Rationalism. As described earlier, civilization needs *Extensive Experience* and *Embedded Rationality* to deal with complex problems. Civilization is rooted in *Life*, not *Disembodied Rationality*.

Even a paramecium "knows" that. It "wants" to live and its species to live, or at least acts that way. *From paramecium to human, we all start with the same goal: Life not just for ourselves but for our kind.*

Bears and raccoons know this. So do springtime toads singing their songs in the evening behind my house each spring. So does your preacher, priest, rabbi, etc.

They all sing the same sort of lyrics: "Come, let us live and help others live." Some just have more diverse vocabularies for diverse survival strategies for diverse situations.

Our origins go back to inherent *Reverence for Life*, and the value and preservation of Life in traditional ethical codes. If Life is not revered and honored, there is nowhere else to begin solving ethical problems either individually or socially.

Unfortunately, however, Oberhauser in Part 2 is not an isolated phenomenon. If in doubt, ask Lt. Waters and his friends in the Part 3 movie. At the end of *Spectre* Bond throws away his gun and he and Madeleine ride off to a life of peace and tranquility. Sometimes, however, killing in order to protect Life never seems to end. Ask Lt. Waters and his friends.

Since Reverence for Life is built into us, it usually dawns on us spontaneously. As with Mr. White, we begin to develop a "conscience", but as time goes on in a polarized society, we face complex problems and need help. Where do we turn for that kind of help?

You don't consult a paramecium or the baby frog who now lives in the stag horn fern on my back deck about problems with your spouse, employer, or the guy who just ran a traffic light and hit your car, or your reading how many million humans died in Genocidal Attacks in the past hundred years. So we need to *Embody*, and *feel* the meaning of Life itself before proceeding. *Who or what inspires us to do that?*

Each of the 5 Scene titles of Part 3 represents a cultural source that helps all of us to meet such challenges and develop *Survival Strategies*. They relate to issues beyond personal survival. They all begin as ways to help us *Live* better and more *Affectively and Effectively* both *Individually* and *Collectively*.

Paul Slovic laments how often the importance of Genocide is diminished by statistics. Recall Stalin? One death is a tragedy, a million is a statistic. For Genocide to become a real factor in our decision making, it has to become *Embodied*. Let's illustrate this: *Numbers and Nerves* has a chapter in which the scattered bones of African Genocide Victims are used to build their memorials, not knowing which bones belong to which bodies or whose. Nothing in *Tears of the Sun* is as blatant as that, but one of its primary goals is similar, to *Embody Genocidal Issues*.

Before a concrete description of the movie, however, it is important to make a few disclaimers. Otherwise, unnecessary debates can distract from primary issues.

Controversies about historical accuracies concerning Nigeria, about the supposed "white man's burden" orientation, or about the place where it belongs in "war movies" can distract from the power of the movie.

Whether 7,000 or 1,000,000 were exterminated in Nigeria during the war described in the movie distracts us into *Numbers*. If the nearly 3,000 exterminated in New York in 9/11 in New York was Genocide, 7,000 can certainly be.

No one disputes that over 1,000,000 were exterminated in Rwanda, so imagine if you like that the movie takes place there. If you are into the issue of "white man's burden", one of Lieutenant Water's brethren is black, and his (and our) growing bond with the blacks of Africa is central to the movie.

The central issue here, as in both earlier movies in this book, is the Embodied development taking place. The problem is humans who have little *Empathy* or *Compassion* for those who suffer, and how it *feels* as such emotions develop. The issue in Part 3 is as simple as that. Those two emotions do not automatically solve every individual let alone complex social problems, but if they are not present, no problem is likely to be solved no matter they are describe otherwise.

If you have not seen the movie already, you may prefer to read my description rather than see it. It is not an easy movie to watch without shedding your own "tears of the sun". It is all a matter of "what you are up for".

Issues concerning Empathy are basic in *both Meet Joe Black* and *Spectre*, but here they are central to deeply painful global issues, and this movie may be as close as most readers will ever get experientially. So brace yourself, here we go.

Lieutenant Waters (played by Bruce Willis) is ordered by the Commander (Tom Skerritt) of an aircraft carrier offshore from Nigeria to rescue from a jungle hospital a "package" including Dr. Lena Kendricks (Monica Bellucci, who plays a cameo role early in *Spectre*). She and her other medical personnel at a mission hospital are about to be overrun by Genocidal Troops who show no more mercy to medical personnel than anyone else.

Like Oberhauser, such terrorists lack Empathy, without which they easily chop off the heads and/or rape innocents. Their only feeling is Violence, the only way they know to achieve power. According to reports of some escapees from the ranks of Genocidal terrorists, new "recruits" before joining they must kill members of their own family (Remind you of Oberhauser?) to demonstrate their "loyalty". That makes it easy without compunction to butcher villagers including children, rape women and/or sell them into sexual slavery, etc.

When Lt. Waters and his team of Navy Seals arrive to rescue the "package", Dr. K is unwilling to go without her tribal friends. Waters refuses at first to consider that, but when she refuses to go, despite his description on what will happen to her if she stays, he finally relents and says she can take any who are ambulatory with them to the helicopter landing spot, and she agrees.

When one of his team asks him privately if he is serious about his offer, contradicting his assignment, he simply says, "What do you think?"

She and her friends leave with Waters and his team for the landing spot. The priest and two nurses stay with those who are not ambulatory. They are treated gruesomely when the terrorists arrive.

When the excursion party reaches the pick-up point, Dr. K realizes that she has been tricked. Waters forces his "package" onto the copter, and she weeps as they take off, leaving her friends behind. However, *Empathy* begins to work on Lt. Waters, especially when they pass over a village where the dead and often dismembered victims lie scattered among destroyed buildings.

Dr. K's weeping becomes uncontrollable, and Waters orders the pilot to turn back to those left behind, that those who cannot get aboard will try with help to make it on foot to the safety of the border. That is how Empathy works, except among terrorist types, Genocidal or otherwise, who have none.

When they land, the only room available is for children, who are loaded on the copters and they leave. Waters, against the commander's orders, starts with his team, Dr. K., and remaining villagers on a hike that will plausibly make it to the border.

When he is asked by his men why he is doing this, he demonstrates what has already been described in this book as the natural tendency of Reason to *follow* rather than precede Action. He says that he doesn't know.

Empathy leaning toward Compassion is developing within him as they continue their trek to the border. When Dr. K tells Waters how she appreciates his saving her life, he still tells her it was just his job, and when she asks him to call her by her first name Lena, he ignores that. However, it is obvious to her and us that his *Empathy* is evolving.

Like Bond, his initial reaction to brutal behavior is Revenge. As they trek through the jungle they pass a village downhill from them being massacred. He and his troop attack, kill the intruders, and save what is left of the village, so making war is as usual a mixed bag

One of his men forces one of the terrorists to look first at what he has done to villagers before killing him. Another of his team discovers that the terrorist he just killed was a pre-adolescent boy. So they appear to be learning, like Bond, that revenge is not always sweet.

Situations can be complex, which will be common for the rest of this book.

The plot here becomes even thicker. One of his men with a tracking instrument tells Waters that they are being pursued by a troop of soldiers. Someone in their own party has apparently been sending a tracking signal.

He confronts the group directly and discovers the culprit, and when he tries to escape kills him, and learns later that the culprit is a friend not only of Dr. K but another member of their entourage who Waters now learns is the young Crown-Prince of the invaded tribe, who has escaped death when his father was killed.

More complications arise. Dr. K reveals that she knew the Crown-Prince was with them, but did not trust Waters earlier with that information. Their relationship is disrupted. He tells her that he wonders what it takes to make her trust him.

She says she is sorry now that she didn't. Her feelings of *Sympathy*, the second stage from *Empathy* toward *Compassion* deepen with this "experience disturbance" in both her and Waters. Experience can be a good teacher, right?

The pursuing troops have guessed now where they are heading, and bigger forces have joined them. They are gaining ground, and will probably catch them before the border. What should he and his men do, since alone they could travel faster and make it to the border easily? He asks them for input.

They too have been learning about the complexity of Empathy and now agree that the mission is no longer a "package". *Empathy* has for them become *Compassion*, and the urge to *do something for* those with whom they feel *Identity*. They will do their best to make it to the border *with* their new friends.

However, as Shakespeare says, the best laid plans don't always work. Ever had that happen for you?

When the border is within sight, a fierce battle takes place. In the chaos, Waters twice saves Lena, as he is now able to call her, but he also loses all but three of his men, to whom he has become even more *Bonded* than when the mission began. War may sometimes be necessary, but at a price.

His face, typical of Willis, barely shows tears, but we know what is happening within him. The sun may weep tears of rain on the jungle, but he mainly weeps inside.

In the nick of time for what is left of the fleeing entourage, two fighter planes arrive from the aircraft carrier and unload incendiary bombs on the pursuing troops.

Those who survive the battle make it across the border as the commander of the carrier, moved now by what Waters has been doing, arrives with *Compassion* of his own, and loads onto the helicopter Waters, his remaining men, and Lena. Wounded, Waters lies against Lena as they fly off toward the aircraft carrier.

Before they leave, those who are rescued thank Waters and his surviving men, promising never to forget them, and tell Lena they will always love her. The tribe dances and chants around their now escaped new Crown-Prince.

The movie demonstrates how it is often a painful progress that leads from Empathy to Compassion.

Have you ever noticed that yourself? The pain in this movie far exceeds that in either of the first two movies in this book, or of most of us, right?

The transitions from Empathy to Compassion are often extremely traumatic, as they are for Lt. Waters, his men, Lena, and the tribe as they survive one crisis after another during their sojourn, surviving which brings them even closer together.

In such a process, the lessons learned usually by others as well as us individually, leads us into the topics of Parts 3 and 4. We all live as individuals but we also live not alone but together. Few of us are so individualistic that we proceed alone. *We have friends with whom we survive together, and that is rarely easy.*

What lies ahead in Parts 3 and 4 are basic characteristics of the Culture to which we belong, which is for us Here and Now.

Since *Tears of the Sun* revolves mainly around the issue of Genocide, other issues about relationships between men and women are also present and will be treated later, but Waters leaning against Lena is a token of issues that open to later Scenes. For Women's issues, consider a book in Recommended Books by Christine Downing, the head of the SDSU department who hired me many years ago. It is a fascinating book.

It may sound like just another Hollywood "happy ending" for Tears of the Sun, but the tribal dance at the end of the movie belongs there. It grounds things in tribal ritual, a subject to be developed in Part 3, Scene 1.

It is not only in imitation of insect and animal life that we dance. Such collective rituals are as natural a development in humans as in other creatures. We are all in that sense children together of our evolutionary and emotional roots as we celebrate our origins.

We are fortunate to be here. So are the toads that sing in my jungle every spring. They certainly sound like it.

Embodied Culture does not necessarily have a self-conscious awareness in its operation. Politicians often fail in their attempts to accomplish that on our behalf. That kind of collective consciousness has its own embodied "neurological" network of art, science, ethics, politics, and religion, each with its own functions resembling very different organs in the Cultural Body. The new No-Culture movement is just another Destruction Movement capable of going nowhere.

Back to Military issues, I've never personally served in the military. The closest I came was during college in the R.O.T.C. during the Korean War, but the war was over by the time I graduated. I was very young during World War II, but I still remember my letters to and from Uncle Noah, who received a medal for such things as placing hand grenades up under German tanks as they rolled over his trench.

Bonnie's uncle Marshall White started as a fighter pilot in the Pacific and became Commander of one of our two Aircraft Carriers entering Tokyo Bay for the surrender that ended World War II. He brought back the Pagoda we now have by our pool.

You may or may not have military experience, but movies like *Tears of the Sun* may be as close as you may ever come to our military history. However, we may need military help today in America with our radical destructionists.

This book started with the mysteries of what *comes to us* spontaneously and without reflection and forethought. It then turned to how *Instincts* emerge as what *dawns on us* develops with relatively little forethought and into our *Body of Cultural Values*.

The 5 Scenes of both Parts 3 and 4 will illustrate how Embodied Cultural "Organs" work in Art, Ethics, Science, Politics, and Religion in creating and maintaining our Cultural Embodiment today. Are you up for that?

PART 3
SCENE 1 EMBODIED ART

Historically, art begins when humans "sing and dance" in their rituals, imitating rituals in the animal world. Neurologically, art begins when primal emotions develop from Pleasure and Pain toward Rituals concerning birth, mating, death and other trials and tribulations common in Life. All of this still *Makes Sense* today, right?

In *Synesthesia*, common in nearly 5% of humans, senses *merge* physically. Music is not just *Heard* but *Seen* in colors and images and *Felt* all over the body, etc. with *Smell* and *Taste*. There are over 100 possible types of synesthesia. Most of us are at least a tad Synesthetic, right? Music we *don't* like can even make us *Cringe*, right? Primal humans and perhaps some artists today are more than borderline synesthetic, but this is only a beginning for the rest of us.

Art can be described as "beautiful" not only for what it is but what it is Not Yet. Art literally and physically *moves* us within, reaching down through conscious reflection and into our deepest *Unconscious* and *Embodied* levels of reality. These levels are common territory for not only the Arts but Religions, the subject of Scene 5. Both are capable of deep emotional *changes* in how (1) *we Sense things and* (2) *what we Do with them.*

Simple illustration: David Lee's large water color painting of white orchids above my big computer screen reminds me when we started buying orchids for our house. I have kept them growing and re-flowering and usually have 10-15 orchids blooming in the bathroom and around the back patio. It all started with that painting. Art propagates itself very easily.

Artists often Anticipate either unconsciously or consciously what will happen in the future in the Minds and/or Bodies of those who Participate (term my friend Arnold Benz loves) *in their works*. They *Engage* us in their work and help us "Mind the Future".

This notion fascinated me while working on my doctoral dissertation, and still does. *Birds of a feather flock together*.

What fascinated me in my doctoral dissertation is how a literary hero or heroine is someone who is no one but can tell us more about everyone than anyone can, so that one can become someone he or she has never been. A bit obtuse perhaps, but you may see what I was trying to say.

Art covers a broad range of embodied results both physically and intellectually. This not only includes the big tropical fish in large aquariums but pretty little goldfish in fish bowls. (I have a soft spot in my heart for goldfish, as you know.) When you think of art this way, art includes not just what is *pleasurable* but inspires you *physically, emotionally, and even reflectively to do things differently*.

How about the car you drive or would like to drive someday. Is it or is it not a work of art *for you*? We used to have a 1987 white Corvette in our garage, but I sold it when it began to make me feel lonely not to have Bonnie with me when I drove it. But since then I finally found and bought a *red* 1988 Corvette, Bonnie's hard to find favorite Corvette color, and I no longer feel alone when I drive it.

Art doesn't have to be all that grand, however. It could be the dinner you put on the table tonight, or that new dress or T-shirt you buy if it makes you *feel* different. This is what I call *the Affect/Effect of Embodied Art*. Such Affect/Effects are found in the chants and dances in primal cultures, cadenced by shouts, instruments like drums, horns, and flutes, clapping of hands, wild costumes, or anything else within reach.

How much have we really changed? The closest we may have come to such art today may not be in art institutes and museums but sporting events or folk, pop, or rock music concerts.

Athletic contests go back to primal times. While in Hawaii for the science symposium that will be described later, I sat for an hour gazing at one of the small boulders used for rock-jumping contests in early Hawaii history in which in an arrangement of such boulders were a "football" field in which the last man standing as competitors leaped from such boulders to others was the *champion*. Sporting events have a very long history.

Such performances may not match exactly the artistic accomplishment of the late Leonard Bernstein's New York Philharmonic performances of Stravinsky's *Rite of Spring* or his own *West Side Story*, but he was able to impress and inspire not only sophisticated music listeners but the construction workers who stopped work and removed their helmets when his body passed by them on the streets of New York City on the way to his burial, a ritual event in itself.

Art encourages *Participation*. I still remember a cartoon from long ago, depicting a normal man walking into a Picasso exhibit in one frame and walking out a Picasso figure in the next.

While living in Michigan, I spent a lot of time in New York City. For my most *embodied* experiences there I recall especially the *Who* concert at the Fillmore East that described in Scene 5 and two different trips to New York *Dionysius in 69*, created by Richard Schechner.

Schechner collaborated often in his productions with Victor Turner, the prominent American anthropologist. Books by both of them are listed at the end of this one.

Turner wrote about *Performance Rituals* in many different eras, from early primal to contemporary theater. Turner distinguished between *Liminality* (emotional, unstructured, but creative) rituals that lead to *Communitas* (structured and socially controllable) performances as Culture evolves from one era to another.

Embodiment

Neither Liminality nor Communitas usually survive for long without the other. A culture needs the Spontaneity and Creativity of *Liminality*, which on one hand cannot last without *Communitas* Structure, yet on the other hand without the creativity and life of *Liminality*, *Communitas* becomes rigid, degenerates into Dementia, and dies. We will come back to this in Scene 5.

Schechner, the dramatist, specialized in the *Liminal*. *Dionysius in 69* therefore was meant to resemble the liveliness of the Dionysius rituals in the early Greek tradition and primal tribal ritual before that, which represents the more visceral and emotional side of Experience, in contrast to Apollo, representing the more ethereal and eternal side.

The classic Dionysius ritual embodies the clash between Life and Death, which in Primal Ritual *involves* dramatic audience Participation.

The Performance Group players (Doesn't a play traditionally involve *play*?) circulate among the audience in the chambers of the "Performance Garage" in various stages of undress, some with "blood" running all over their bodies. Chants, music, and drumbeats can be heard. The scene is very "vivacious" as you may imagine, and the script allows spontaneous variations, in which the "audience" *Participates* directly.

Illustration: I am approached by a barely dressed and "bloody" actress, who bluntly asks me: "What are you doing tonight?" Unsure whether she meant *during* the performance (taking off clothes, etc.), or *after* the play, (meeting with Schechner and cast, etc.), I reply: "What do you have in mind?" She replies quickly: "A man who does not answer a question with a question," and moves away.

So much for my role as a walk-on performer. There I go, playing a stage-hand again.

It was a typical piece of primal ritual magnified, an effort to bring audience Participants into the "tribe", which fascinated Turner till his death and still fascinates Schechner, although I've had no contact with him for a long while.

The performances were different each time, depending in part on the audience, and were not always very coherent. The ritual reportedly once came unraveled when an audience member (not me) ran away with "Dionysius", and never came back, so the cast had to innovate as best they could to bring everything back together again.

Platonic tradition generally discounted visceral Dionysius in favor of more detached and eternal Apollonian *Desire*. For Plato the Earthly Eros (as in "Erotic") is usually *Momentary and Passing*, but the Eternal Eros is *Philosophical and Lasting*. This leads eventually to the dualistic history of Medieval Christianity until the Renaissance, when Nature and Science became central, but *still operated on laws and standards fixed eternally*. More about that in later Scenes.

At the turn of the 20th Century changes began to take place: (1) *Chance or chaos* surrounds everything that arises, so get used to it, (2) *Non-Linear* orientation arises in which neither time nor space proceed in what might be called straight lines, (3) Reality *Betwixt and Between* things like *Subject (Self)* and *Object (Other) fades as we become Involved*, (4) Relational and Dynamic processes move toward often uncertain goals, (5) Reality is potentially Creative and Unpredictable. Other themes could be listed, but these are surely among the basics.

The old orientation is: (1) Chaos gradually disappears as eventually everything becomes explainable, (2) the rate of change is constant, following a straight line, (3) Reality is *in* things, not the spaces *betwixt and between* them, (4) Things themselves are moved *by* rules and laws, rather than the other way around, (5) Creativity is a name for what we are not yet able to explain.

Embodiment

Such notions are as basic to Arts as to Science. *Look at, listen to, feel, or read any of the works of art created by the following artists, and you will discover what these mean.* Each art is "scaffolded" by all five themes.

Composer Igor Stravinsky, painter Pablo Picasso, poet T.S. Eliot, and novelist James Joyce all begin with Elemental Chaos and the undoing of what was Linear and into a strange kind of Synchronicity that brings all five themes together. Stravinsky's *Rite of Spring* is a ritual-oriented musical performance introducing us to the age in which we live.

I've six recordings of the *Rite of Spring* with five different conductors and their orchestras performing them, including Stravinsky. To me Leonard Bernstein's New York Philharmonic performance in 1957 is still the best. It's Chaotic, Nonlinear, Multi-perspective, Dynamically Interactive, and Creative like nothing before it. Listen and you'll *Hear* and *Feel* it rather than having to think *about* it.

Picasso does very similar things in his paintings. He, like Stravinsky, created riots in the streets of Paris when his first cubist paintings appeared. But *look* at them and you will *see* the five themes for yourself. They *Affect/Effect* you directly. Recall the cartoon depicting first a normal looking man walking into a Picasso exhibit, then walking out looking like a Picasso figure. What do you suppose he does next?

Eliot and Joyce are more abstract and not easily read without help, although the 5 themes are there just to look at them on black and white pages. For unraveling their ambiguities, you may need secondary sources to understand either of them in depth. Richard Ellmann at Northwestern helped me with both Eliot and Joyce.

Many books that include Eliot's *Wasteland* include commentaries. Joyce's *Finnegans Wake* is an extremely complex tale of someone who wakes up during his own funeral *Wake*. The Joseph Campbell book listed in Recommend Books unravels the *Wake*. The gist of our Arts today begin here. What is Dead Arises!

A final note about artistic *Performance*. My friend Sheridon Stokes retired recently from his 40 year experience in the music department at UCLA, during which he *composed* music and *performed* in major orchestras and Hollywood Movies. (His wife Shelley was a close friend of Bonnie's from their Point Loma, San Diego school days.)

Sheridon several years ago drew me aside for a walk-on performance far easier for me to do than in an actress once offered me during the performance of *Dionysius in 69*, the *Affect/Effect* of which obviously lingered with me for many years.

Sheridan invited me to perform as a bass soloist during a fund raising event in their home for the "little ballerinas and their tutus" for the California Ballet Company before the Gala Season Performance of one of his works. I respond immediately, not wanting to fail another possible walk-on performance. I composed with my own words a song to the recording of Swan Ballet in which I pleaded for money from well-to-do folks for the little ballerinas.

This time it does not require anything as adventurous as taking off my clothes, but I do get down on my knees once, begging as I sing before an older man who I could see had a checkbook in his shirt pocket. To my surprise he responds quickly to my offer (shades of Dionysius in 69). Tears come to his eyes, he takes out his checkbook and writes me a check, which became widely applauded as the climax of my act.

I swear that this is all true, but I learn later that he is a famous character actor in Hollywood movies, so he actually up-staged me, and I am again a stage hand.

My performance is a big hit in any case, and afterward the director of the company invites me to participate at the beginning of opening segment of their show by singing three German art songs while his young ballerinas dance around me "in their new tutus". It is a great success for both me and the little ballerinas as we bow together at the end of our performance.

So even stage-hands can have their day. To me it was right up there with walking out into swirling swans and geese on the levies at Shiawassee Flats. And besides that, I am finally successful as a walk-on performer except that this time I was one of them. Every dog has its day, as Rafe has already demonstrated.

Of course we don't necessarily have to limit such things to one day. *Life is a stage*, as Shakespeare says in *Macbeth*. Any day can be that kind of day, right?

PART 3
SCENE 2 EMBODIED ETHICS

Scenes 1 and 5 are obviously Bottom-Up and Emotional in origin. Scene 2 on Ethics and 3 on Science *appear* to be Top-Down and Rational in origin, yet even they rely on Bottom-Up and Experiential sources that are not at first obvious.

Philosophical ethics tends to begin at the Top of things with laws and rules while ignoring the *Origins* of these laws and rules. It is better to begin with the Nature of Life itself if you really want to understand Ethics.

For the 2017 annual meeting in Hawaii of the American Association for the Advancement of Science, Pacific Division, I wrote a paper and presentation titled "Neurological Origins for a Scientific Ethic". The collection of papers, including mine, has since then been published by Nova Science.

In short, the case that I make there and here is that Ethics either there or here or elsewhere in both Ethics and Science begins with Nature and for us humans the Neurology it has been developing since very early in our Enviromental History.

The *Bible* says God expected Cain to know better than to kill Abel long before the 10 Commandments appeared.

Ethics actually begins in the very origins of Life, in which Everything is a matter of Life and Death both physically and socially. As you have gathered already, these ethical roots are found in our origins in animal life long before humans appear on earth. Bears for example were here millions of years before humans.

We even see the origin of ethics in the single-celled life of the lowly paramecium, who flees wildly when facing threats to life, and also self-propagate spontaneously to produce new paramecia. Ethics therefore concerns Survival of not only ourselves but our kind. Whether this is Intentional depends on your definition of Intentional, but in terms of Pragmatic Results, these traits are Ethical.

When we hatch from mommy's womb, our evolutionary heritage provides Survival Strategies for more and more complex situations related to Life and Death, which become in turn scaffolding upon which we build both individual and social ethical structures, following what we learn from a paramecium. We just have 100 billion more neurons to handle more complex problems than a paramecium is equipped to handle, but *this* gets us started.

This does not solve automatically what faces Lena, Lt. Waters, and their friends in *Tears of the Sun*, but does help to get a *Grip for* what they face. *Terrorist/Genocidalists* an for that matter Destructionists generally have no *grip* at all. All they know how to do is Destroy things, as in many urban supposedly peaceful "protests" lately.

Granted that we need more than getting an ethical grip, basic Neurology teaches us even more. *As Antonio Damasio says, our billions of Neurons "Mind the Future" as we process through the myriad of the Interactions of Neuron Populations within us. These interactions include the development of such emotions as Empathy and Compassion that build on what Damasio once called Supra-Instinctive Survival Strategies.*

Such strategies blend naturally toward a Social-Moral point of view that transcends immediate individual interests in formulating a Culture beyond Tribal concerns as we move into bigger and bigger worlds.

As in Genesis, Commandments would make no sense anyway for someone who has lost that Grip. God learns from the *Smell* of blood what Cain has done. *Lesson: Our senses teach us a lot if we make Good Sense with them. Ethics then emerges not out of Abstract Thought but out of Common Sense.*

This begins with how we bring the world from Outside to Inside us, which is far more complex Ethically than Top-Down approaches realize.

The following quotation comes not from a famous scholar but my old war veteran friend Biker Mike: *"We have to honor the equipment we are riding. It is part of us."*

Ever known a biker? Mike never convinced me to buy a Harley, but when I bought my first old Corvette, he conceded that it was the next best thing to "ride". He gave me rides on his old Harley; I gave him rides in my old Corvette.

If you have a real piece of equipment, it is part of you, like your body is. This is Biker Mike's lesson for us all.

Keeping what Mike said in mind reminds us that we are deeply interlinked with our surroundings generally, and to take that a step deeper: *Our neurons are our link to our surroundings as they bring those surroundings inside us.*

We are *Interactive Agents* in neurological processes that also include chemical components such as genes, hormones and neuromodulators traveling in the blood stream, but the Heart of Ethical Processing is in *Neurons*, whether stimulating or stimulated by chemical inputs.

Neurons, as Damasio says, always "Mind the Future" in our Neurological Systems as we process the myriad of interactions between and among Populations of Neurons eventuating in the development of such emotions as Empathy and Compassion, Supra-Instinctive Survival Strategies, and eventually our Cultural Values.

If we get this Grip from animals, do animals behave ethically? They do have an ethical language of sorts perhaps. Remember the cartoon of an Eskimo telling a friend that his husky now knows 40 words, although most of them mean snow, so my comment was that it may be the Eskimo whose vocabulary is limited. He has only one word for snow. Snow like water may also have many meanings, right? Ask a husky.

Allow me therefore to ask you: Could Momma Raccoon be considered not only a good mother but *Ethical* in her care of her Special Child? She seemed at least close to that, right? So where does maternal "instinct" for either animals or humans *end* and ethics *begin*?

When Damasio describes complex animals, he includes such feelings as sympathy, attachments, and submission. Have you noticed any of these traits in your pets?

Momma raccoon illustrates embarrassment, dominant pride, and humble submission. Granting that cats, or at least mine, are not very good at embarrassment or submission, they certainly experience *attachment*. Mother Raccoon seems to experience all of them, although her special child is still far away from complex feelings described by Damasio.

What about fathers? Each morning I look out at the humming-bird feeder to see Papa Hummingbird guarding the feeder for what I take to be his family, but turn others away from "his bowl", so to speak. I mean, give us parents some ethical credit, bird or beast.

Damasio credits Baruch Spinoza, whom Peirce also admired for *his fascinating understanding of the relationship between emotion and ethics*. Damasio finds Spinoza's theories incomplete, but feels he is on the right track.

Damasio himself does a beautiful job of blending Neurobiology into Culture and its social ethics. So does Andy Clark, who appreciates Damasio's books but has his own Embodied Cognitive Science approach, which is similar and even more deeply involved in the latest neurological research concerning our Culture.

Damasio speaks more concretely about Culture than any other neurobiologist, but like others is unable to locate more than very generally *where Neurology ends and Ethics begins*, which leaves us with the conclusion that their edges still cannot ultimately can be separated.

I've been thinking about Albert Schweitzer lately and his motto: *Reverence for life*. Half a century ago Schweitzer ended up in Africa, not all that far from where *Tears of the Sun* takes place. Could reading Schweitzer be part of what takes Lena and her husband there?

Unfortunately, of course, humans are sometimes warped ethically by things that are rarely found in animals, like hate, greed, addictions, corruptions, indoctrinations, and genocidal motivations. Then we have something far worse than a human pig-wallow on our hands.

Even mothers are not always right about everything. Consider my mother's paranoia about pigs and the way she yanked me out of the pig-wallow. It wasn't her fault she had been *Indoctrinated* about dirt. Read Brett and Arietta's *Let Them Eat Dirt* and you will see what I mean.

Mr. White in *Spectre* says his conscience has grown, as it apparently did for the Apostle Paul when witnessing mass murders taking place. So again, Conscience is not just a Top-Down Guilt product. For Mr. White's Conscience seems to arise Naturally from his Experience.

What we should do arises Naturally *out of Experience*. Consider *Tears of the Sun*. Who did what is "right" when the terrorists approach the mission compound? Consider the priest, the nurses, Dr. K, Lt. Waters, and his men. If you were in such a situation, what would you do? It's complicated, isn't it?

No standard ethical system can speak more than vaguely for *any* of them. The characters in *Tears of the Sun* face different situations, have different orientations, and are different humans. Ethics can often be ambiguous can't it, even *with* ethical codes and systems? In the end, it is often left up to *you*, like those in *Tears of the Sun*, to decide what is the most ethical thing to do. *You often Create the Ethics.*

The doctor/priest has disabled patients, and doesn't want to leave them to be slaughtered *alone*, so he stays, as do both of the nurses. Dr. K has the ambulatory to consider, including the fleeing president-elect, but can't tell Lt. Waters about that. Lt. Waters knows his responsibility is to rescue his "package", but is already stifling his feelings about the "package" and even what it *is*. So are his comrades in arms.

Look how their Ethical Sensitivity develops during their Experiences as they bring the Outside World Inside them. They all have far more painful and even lethal emotional decisions to make far more complex to face than Joe Black or James Bond ever have.

What would *you* do if you were the younger nurse? Her two much older colleagues were already committed to staying, but what if you or I had been in her shoes, what would we do? Complicated isn't it?

In many decisions we humans have to make, how strange it is that we have to Create the right thing to do rather than decide based on abstract standards.

This is where Ethics becomes more than a matter of obeying either your conscience or any set of ethical rules or regulations. You often need to dig deep within your consciousness in order to discover what is Ethical for you as the unique human you are. Makes Life both scary and interesting, doesn't it?

Commandments may *fit more* situations than folk heuristics, but like them, they have demonstrated in practice that they work well in given situations. However, it requires more than Commandments to tell the priest, the nurses, Dr. K, or Lt. Waters what to do next. Lena learns only *through Experience*, for example, that she *should* have trusted Waters, etc.. etc., etc.

SCENE 3 EMBODIED SCIENCE

Scene 1 describes five themes found in the arts and sciences of the early 20th centuries: (1) Chance or chaos surrounds everything that arises, so get used to it, (2) Non-linear orientation, neither time nor space proceeding in straight lines, (3) Reality as *Betwixt and Between* things, multi-causal and multi-perspective, (4) Relational and Dynamic Processes, moving in uncertain directions, (5) Reality as Creative, new things often appearing unpredictably.

This scene could follow all those themes in science rather than art, but numerous references have already described scientists from Darwin through Einstein and current movements like Dynamic Complex Systems and Embodied Cognitive Science.

Since we have already been there and done that in several places concerning Science, this Scene will pick up the subject of the last Scene, Embodied Ethics, and relate it to Embodied Scientific Ethics.

It is easy for any of us to become lost in momentary processes and lose track of our ethical origins, which go back through cuttlefish to single-celled paramecium operating unconsciously and spontaneously for the Survival Strategies of its kind, as described earlier.

Scientists and Technologists, like the rest of us, are busy thinking about tons of things, and all too often lose touch with their surroundings. So scientists and technologists often don't think in any broader contexts than the rest of us usually do. It is a matter of what has to be done *today* in order to keep *our* jobs, projects, or professional futures running. Although we should all be smarter than a paramecium, are we?

Scientists involved in medicine and environment may be exceptions, but even there, it is all too easy to fall into "dog eat dog" competitive *Survival of the Fittest* rather than what *Fits the Survival of us all*, based on our Origins.

Embodiment

C. S. Peirce warned us that Power and Greed are too often found in the very roots of life itself. It doesn't take long for Adam and Eve or any of us to "go astray". Much of this is due to what could be called general *Myopia*, Short-Sightedness.

With far more neurological research available than Peirce, Walter Freeman calls this Solipsistic Isolation. It begins with the legitimate and understandable awareness of *Uniqueness*, described elsewhere in this book. However this can be warped into *Solipsistic Isolation*, Uniqueness gone mad *without* the balancing act of Others, which Kauffman calls *Private Meaning* without real *Public Involvement*.

When we are preoccupied with the former, the latter suffers, so if we don't see *behind* or *beyond* us, we surely don't see the world of Others *around* us. This applies not only to Oberhauser in *Spectre* but the pursuing terrorists in *Tears of the Sun*.

Survival both individually and collectively means more than surviving till the next paycheck or achievement. Power and Greed is a bad way to maintain our motivations, right? So with the danger of *Solipsistic Isolation*, we *need* to recall the Importance of Survival Collectively and Collaboratively in what in this book has been called our *Survival Strategies*.

Back for a few moments to the symposium I described earlier that my friend Jay Raghavan and I organized for the *American Association of Science, Pacific Division* on the big volcano island of Hawaii. Despite the volcano attraction, the general numbers of scientists involved in these conferences has been declining for years. Jay and I had one of the few symposiums that had enough good paper proposals to fill a full day. The morning session was fairly well attended. However, the afternoon attendance fell dramatically, mostly because attendees apparently went out to see the live volcano or whatever, despite other days set aside for that.

It was especially embarrassing concerning one paper by a very prominent afternoon presenter. His afternoon paper was only because he needed equipment that was not available in the morning. Alas, although his afternoon paper was announced as the first in the afternoon, hardly anyone was there to see and hear him. Fortunately, we at least included him in the published papers.

Myopia and Solipsistic Isolation also showed to early 20^{the} century psychologists when they oversimplified *Human Perception* into a far too mechanical *Stimulus-Response*. Since then we have learned otherwise neurologically, psychologically, philosophically, and socially.

Maurice Merleau-Ponty, whom I studied in graduate school in the philosophy rather than psychology department at Northwestern, made it clear that even basic Perception is an *Active*, not a *Passive* and *Mechanical* process. (1) The perceiver actively carries *into* perception far more than is obvious, and (2) The response carries far more *out of it* than is obvious.

This may Seem to have little to do with Ethics as such, but it illustrates of how even Science sometimes fails when it *thinks* it has a good picture of things and has left too much out of the picture. That is why I also make a point to include painting and pictures on my walls at home with no frames.

Put in terms of the *frame problem*, establishing a "frame" within which to work may have obvious practical advantages, because it is much easier to solve a problem where there are fewer variables to consider. Often that works, but not always. Algorithms and data often work *within* complicated frames, but those frames risk leaving things out that later are important.

Nature progresses without frames at all and yet over time makes noticeable progress. That does not mean that we need to stop using frames. We usually have time and efficiency factors to consider, where nature usually has all the time it wants. With us there is always the question, however, of what are we leaving out of our equations in the *really* big picture.

Although Nature proceeds without frames, it has lots of time to process the relative wisdom or foolishness of its efforts. We often *don't* have that much time, so we need to be reminded of what we may have left out of consideration when we do things.

Now return again to the AAAS-Pacific Division's Hawaii symposium, this time to our papers. When considering our Scientific Ethics papers, there are two traditional scientific problems to consider: (1) Where things come *from* and (2) where they are *going*.

The symposium papers therefore focused on (1) *prior ethical grounding before whatever a theory or product leaves home*, or (2) *subsequent results when the rubber hits the road and Results need to be reviewed that need review in a broader context.*

Most of the papers deal with (2), subjects like how many species are disappearing every day, the unpredictable consequences of technology, human rights assessments, the international dynamics of "birthing agents and surrogacy", large scale famine, all of which are very important subjects. My paper dealt with (1), the neurological and experiential roots of *any* Scientific Ethic.

It included the following: As a recent illustration of (1), Paul Slovic's *Affect Heuristic* starts with scientific method itself. As reported earlier, Slovic was already an expert in Risk Management statistics, but as reported earlier, one day when he was about to cross the street on foot in heavy traffic, he realized that whole field of risk management was ignoring the *emotional* components of risk.

As a result, his work has changed the very nature of Risk Management research in widely diverse fields such as Advertising and Genocide studies, the latter a theme in *Tears of the Sun*. What Paul Slovic calls *Affect Heuristic* actually relates to all science, including Scientific Ethics.

You may recall that Joseph Stalin said that one death is a tragedy but a million deaths is a statistic. Valuable as the numbers of statistics may be, it is easy to get lost in them, which is obvious in

Numbers and Nerves, listed in Recommended Books. *Put in Antonio Damasio's language, numbers in themselves do not "sense the future" the way neurons do.*

As Damasio puts it, the entire neurological system is forever *Sensing the Future* and ultimately matters of *Supra-Instinctive Survival Strategies*. Neurons are not just out-board ride-alongs. They are at the heart of what the entire system is designed *for*.

Example of a project illustrating all this: In *Science*, the weekly journal of the *American Association for the Advancement of Science, Human Genome Modification*, a prominent ethical issue in Neurobiology today blends nicely with both (1) and (2) described above, including (1) a quote from Albert Schweitzer, to whom I return in Scene 5, that *all* ethics is based on a sense of Human Solidarity in Ethical Values, beginning with Life itself.

In 1975 in Asilomar, California scientists had recommended strict safeguards insuring that Human Gene Lines *not* be modified in DNA research. Since then, however, many things have become possible concerning Survival Issues.

Methods unavailable earlier have emerged in Prenatal Genetic Diagnosis, and it's now within reach for children who otherwise would be born with genetic defects can be born healthy.

Although this is a dramatic *Survival Issue*, however, the new procedures have possible "flies in the genetic oatmeal" in *Off-Target Effects*, like *Unintentional* production of children perhaps susceptible to worse problems than whatever is prevented, *or* Hitler-type scientists could engage in *Intentional* efforts to create "superior" human beings. So the problem includes both (1) and (2) issues.

You can see here how complicated Scientific Ethics can become in producing acceptable Affect/Effects, right?

Scientific Research requires very complex feedback processes, some of which are beyond statistic factors. Meanwhile hopeful parents stand in waiting lines alongside disability rights advocates, ethicists, and other specialists become involved in considering such things considering such categories as "never", "maybe but only if ….", etc.

Know what this reminds me of? The situation facing those at the mission hospital in *Tears of the Sun*. The primary difference there is that they are not just facing the survival of those in the mission hospital but their personal orientations concerning this.

Perhaps it is one of those situations in which no set of standards or principles can answer the problem for everybody. We are in a place where we have to *Create* what is the right thing to do. Time is the only test of what works, and that is often vague ahead of time.

In short, we have to Create whatever we do and be able to live with it. That is not always fun, but it is what we have to do if we want to do what is Ethical, whether as scientist or any other kind of human being. Sometimes scientists have to make decisions, but other times the individuals have to do that.

Science is doing revolutionary things today, and it moves with feedback systems the complexity of which resembles what the human neurological system always does for a living, developing Supra-Instinctive Survival Strategies that have (2) good results without losing track of (1) the general counsel of Albert Schweitzer, that *Reverence for Life* is at the root of all Science, Ethics, and Life. Usually that works in the long run.

PART 3
SCENE 4 THE BODY POLITIC

This title originated long ago when a king was said to have two bodies, his physical body and his kingdom. We no longer have such kings nor consider ourselves the body of a king. Even where kings and queens exist today, most of them play more integrated roles with their people.

Most of us Americans perceive ourselves together as *Embodied*, and we only need a collective and collaborative *"head"* to help *us* govern things as we see them. Unfortunately at this moment our two political parties are Polarized and tearing *us* apart. Hopefully that will change before the upcoming election or soon after. *In short, we can accept two Parties, but not two Countries.*

As you know, honeybees have a society that for ages has run quite well without an official *head* at all except for queen bee, whose only power is laying zillions of eggs. Politicians in this country are so Polarized today, they rarely hatch. I don't mean to insult *all* politicians, because we have politicians in both parties whose eggs have hatched and resulted in great things, but rarely now.

In reading this book, you know already that I am a Pragmatist, and given the way I treasure my open-countryside upbringing, I am also a Populist of sorts, *but* I am for years now neither Democrat nor Republican although I've been each of them for long periods.

The primary problem today in America is our *Polarization*, which leaves our President Trump or Obama before him taking advantage of "executive privilege" to run things himself. As claimed by Daniel Henninger recently in WSJ, since neither polarized party is strong enough to get much done, the President does it *for us.*

President Trump is fortunately a Pragmatist with some clear-cut Results, *but* he is also a Top-Down operator with *"Foot in Mouth*

Disease", rudely attacking his opponents and offending many voters who now think him too "uncivilized" to be our President.

Nearly as rude, Leftist Ideologists (locked to certain beliefs and principles) suffer from *"Shoot Everybody in Both their Feet Disease"*, including their own Moderates who have made Democrat current control of the House of Representatives possible.

Although the Right has fewer Ideologists, it often suffers from "Shoot Yourself in the Foot Disease", only recently producing legislation of their own different from what the President wants.

Meanwhile Ideological (some call this Fake) News commentators belly-ache endlessly, convincing nobody but themselves they are right.

What happens to the Body Politic? It is left in pieces on the ground, Disembodied.

First, The Body Politics is split between Top and Bottom, as *Everything in Politics becomes a Top-Down power operation.*

Second, The Body Politic is split down the middle, the two parties no longer with any way to *talk*, let alone *work with* each other. *The traditional Balancing Act of our Founders, who also often disagreed vigorously with each other, is gone.*

Third, The Ideological News channels only make things worse with their mudslinging. This "helps" the Spirit of the 21st Century?

Who can really help put this Humpty and Dumpty back together again? One answer can be found in the roots of the Body Politic who have now learned what works and what does not and no longer believe empty political promises. Such promises mean nothing if they cannot already show Results somewhere, which Ideologists are rarely able to do, meanwhile claiming of course that their own failures are really the other party's.

A great possible Bottom-Up solution arises with a recent survey showing that 43% of the Public identifies itself as neither Right or Left, so this "Invisible Political Body" is actually our biggest "Party". Where is our News Channel?

What "Dawns on Me Now" is that this Invisible Political Body Is potentially "The Spirit of the 21st Century". Like the Supposedly Nothing that to Merleau-Ponty holds Polarities together is (again) Not Really Nothing. We too may not be all that obvious, but we can Vote to have Polar Affect/Effects land where we want them.

Far Right and Left Radicals often think of us as weak and uncertain, so they need to "instruct" (meaning "brainwash") us. This is the biggest pile of Cow Manure since barns were invented. *We just have enough Common Sense to measure things by Results rather than Empty Promises, so We decide which Politicians and Policies we can "Have Confidence In" for Results (See Part 4, Scene 2), not their Promises and/ or what they Say or Think.*

So please allow me to say: *We Invisibles are sick and tired of Whining Ideots (abbreviation for Ideologists) otherwise known as Talking Disembodied Heads* (not to be confused with *Idiots, who may be saints, so please note the difference in spelling*).

Let Ideots rave (as long as they do not become physically Violent, which they've done lately and belong permantly in jail). Ironically, outside of cheating on votes, which Ideots are more than willing to do, they still have little to do with who wins any elections.

No matter how you registered, have you ever considered a split ticket; there are a few fine candidates on both sides. Of course that drives Ideots crazy. How Sad!

To change our conversation back to *Embodiment* that begins with Living, not Dead, Neurons, this fits us Embodied Voters as a Living but currently Invisible Body Politic. A Head can do nothing important today without such a Bottom-Up Body, except to Destroy things.

A physical body is well integrated both top and bottom, side by side. The old expression is about how the right hand doesn't know what the left is doing. If we are Alive, ours really do, just as my right hand knows better than my brain when looking for what I dropped somewhere on the messy bed beside me some time long before going to sleep. Trust *yourself* more than any Ideot politician.

Politicians too often (but fortunately not always) resemble the lion, supposedly King of the Beasts, who kills his own cubs so the lionesses will have to mate with him to have more cubs. Even Ideological Politicians don't do exactly that of course, but the question for both lion and politician is: *Who is being served, the served or the server?* Ideologists usually serve themselves more than those they promise to serve.

Ignore their Promises and look at their Records. The Records of Ideologists are unimpressive. Ask anybody who lives in Venezuela. If Ideots get what Ideologically *they* want, despite their promises, those voting for them won't. It *always* happens that way.

Some (not all of course) politicians may be eating *our* money rather than our children, although even that is not obvious when Ideologists plan to close Charter Schools, as described in Part 4, Scene 4.

This doesn't mean we Invisibles have no differences, even big ones. However, we are *not* attacking each other Violently, always the method of Ideologists. We're just Friends voting differently. *We still Live on the same street in a Functional Neighborhood.* Americans have a long history of collaborating well with each other, even when the chips are down. *It is a matter of the American Spirit.*

Representative Steve Scalise of Louisiana was delivering a speech to congress on his first day on the job after over 3.5 months of hospitalization after being shot and nearly killed during, of all things, a charity softball game between Democrats and Republicans. *It is almost as if the shooter couldn't tolerate seeing the two Parties having fun together.*

Scalise is given a long, standing ovation by both parties. His speech was very moving in calling Democrats and Republicans to come together to address the issues of our day. Both side party leaders obviously appear to agree with what he says.

Great idea, but talk is cheap! If they can play baseball, why can't they do it in the political game? Nobody's life is on the line here. Or is it?

A recurring theme in this book is that dramatic change often occurs when we are pressed to our limits. Well, the Life of our Body Politic (Spirit of the 21st Century) is on the line.

Consider Victor Turner, an anthropologist whose influence has become widely influential in recent decades. Culture (as well as individual lives) tend for him to proceed in two positive stages that follow the negative one: *Alienation*: (1) *Liminality*, "Threshold" processes that often evolve in lively and creative ways, but unfortunately by itself, Liminality cannot last, so (2) *Communitas*, "Structure", is necessary for enduring cultural survival. But if political "structure" ages and becomes rigid (Ideological), Life disappears and it dies, unfortunately sometimes Violently.

In his later work he divides Communitas into *Spontaneous* and *Ideological*. Put bluntly, the former is Alive, the latter is Dead. *For a political illustration, deciding who is guilty before the trial begins is Dead even before it starts and smells like it to us Invisibles.*

Our culture politically now is loaded with Turner's *Ideological Communitas*. This Never Ever works. *Our Culture will inevitably Die unless we do something about it. That of course is what they want. Is it what you want?*

Seems to me what is locked in the same old places Ideologically leads to *Premature Rigor Mortis*, which slowly seeps from the top down, as in *Dementia* among many of the "elderly". *As you may know, people with Rigor Mortis are incapable of handling Living problems.* They do not communicate well with anybody, and certainly don't govern well.

Even people with premature *Rigor Mortis*, however, may still become Violent. Call it the *Revenge of the Zombies* or *Night of the Living Dead*. All hell breaks loose, and everything degenerates into chaos when election time approaches. This is pretty much American politics today, especially some big cities, right?

When will Everybody or at least 43% of us Come to our Senses? Who knows? In the "for what it is worth" department, which is to say "Have some Confidence In" as described in Part 4, Scene 2, *America has a new age ahead of us that will be Neither Far Right Nor Far Left.*

Evidence: When such chaos has occurred earlier in American history, it is usually the good old Body Politic with the help of a few *Embodied* Politicians who rise above the chaos.

Consider the Democrat Joe Lieberman's major WSJ article on radical Democrat reactions to Trump's killing General Solemani when they had cheered Obama's killing Ben Laden. Most Democrats seem to have "forgotten" this, but Bless Lieberman's heart for reminding us.

Any neurological system that behaves as ineptly as current American politics would be dead already, but fortunately there are signs of Life here and there, such as the President's temper softening somewhat, and Democrats getting tired of efforts to impeach him, at least before the up-coming election. But so far that isn't much, but time between now and the election will tell our tale.

Trump is very *unlikely* to suddenly become a "civilized" and "foot out of his mouth" person. Biden is *unlikely* to suddenly stand up against the Left wing Radicals. *In whom do we Have Confidence to continue and improve earlier Results they've had.* The test will be whether any *unlikely* factors can be *erased by election time.*

In any case we will see what happens, and hope we can in the process maintain the *Spirit of the Twenty First Century*, no matter which Party wins. *As stated at the beginning of this Scene, we can accept having two Parties, but not living in two Countries.*

PART 3
SCENE 5 EMBODIEDRELIGION

Primal artistic-religious rituals imitate animal and even insect rituals. Consider ritual bird calls in the morning, evening, or night, and wolves howling at the moon at the end of *Dances with Wolves*. Young Jesse is not the only one inspired by the moon. If you "give a hoot", as Hoosiers say, ask any owl about this. Such things could be called *the Religion of Animals*.

As it develops, Religious Ritual becomes distinctive in its ability to bring loose ends together in order to Enthuse humans to function socially with a sense of "well being". As a Rumanian Orthodox Christian scientist told my friend Arnold Benz, science and religion conflict there is rare since "religion is more a way of spirituality."

For Nassim Taleb religion is founded on Participation, especially Rituals, focusing on creating and maintaining what he calls *Antifragility* in an obviously *Fragile* world. "Beliefs" themselves are Fragile today, yet Rituals today have been tested for thousands of years, including very Fragile times, so probability is that they will continue to work today. He himself is Eastern Orthodox so he focuses in his attention on Experience rather than Doctrine.

Plato tried to solve emotional problems by concentrating on *Desire (Eros)* with a bottom-up approach, and for centuries it worked. The religious world of the "Middle Ages" declared that the pain and grief of Earthly Desire could be absorbed into the Eternal Love of God, so you may die on earth but won't in heaven.

Nice package, but a few centuries later the Renaissance and Modern Science explain Everything not in heavenly but earthly terms. This resulted in what some now call the Secular Age. In two 900 page books, Charles Taylor details elaborate historical descriptions of the rise of Secularity and its various spin-offs.

The anthropologist Victor Turner has a simpler and more general description of major cultural transformations, including how both individual and cultural *Rites of Passage* develop historically from *Liminality* (Threshold) to *Communitas* (Incorporation). If he were still alive, he might claim that the Secular *age* is part of a Liminal *transition*, but not *Communitas*.

Jesus was two thousand years ago a rather *Liminal* guy, not traditional at all, hanging out with a diverse crowd with not just religious types, but fishermen, tax collectors, women at wells, former prostitutes, etc. He was *not* an Ideologue. He focused on experience and parables. Like Jesus, we live in another *Threshold (Liminal)* period. Any *Structure* that will Survive may need deeper roots than Secularity or Ideologies can possibly provide.

Over a century ago C. S. Peirce speaks of a different kind of Love from that of Plato, one that is grounded in Evolutionary Process. He speaks, as do Damasio and James Bond in *Spectre*, of *Instinct*, not as an *unlearned, pre-packaged drive*.

Peirce develops no traditional argument for God's "Existence", which he considers a useless logical category. Instead he advances his "Neglected Argument" not for God's "*Existence*" but for God's *Reality*.

Peirce introduces a new category *Abduction* alongside *Induction* and *Deduction*, both of which to him concern a hypothesis that has *already* become definable. *Abduction concerns how a hypothesis arises in the first place, which is Pragmatic and Experiential.*

You could say that for Peirce Love rather than Conflict is what makes the world go around, meaning that Love is what Bonds rather than Alienates humans as well as the rest of the world with one another.

Love for Peirce has three stages: (1) *Actuality*, the appearance of many-things from no-things, (2) *Possibility*, the *interaction* of things with each other, and (3) *Survival* or *Decay*, which is how Evolutionary

Embodiment

Love makes a Living, right up to you when your mommy's hatch opens and you pop out, a Love Child.

To Peirce this is how *The Gospel of John* describes God as Light, Life, and Love. John grants that no one has ever seen God, yet (1) a Light (Reality) is turned on that leads to (2) Interactive Life (Possibility) that (3) results in either Destiny (Decay) or Love (Inspired Collaboration and Creativity).

Peirce is not claiming of course that every skunk loves its pups the same way your mommy loves you. There are various levels of all three Stages, but this is not where to elaborate details, except to say that each set of three has three more sets of three, etc.

Genesis, like John, begins Evolution with the "waters of the deep" and the appearance of (1) *Light*, leading to developing (2) complexities of *Life during* each passing day and then (3) *Love* between Adam and Eve, etc.

Such Transformations usually begin with Crisis of some sort, as in *Meet Joe Black*, *Spectre*, and *Tears of the Sun*, or when the Apostle Paul falls off his horse. Its Stages often take a lot of time to complete. For Paul it takes years of Experience to write I Corinthians 13.

But stay for now with the broader meaning of Transformations, which I call *Transmogrifications*, and go back to what Turner calls *"painfully achieved modalities of experience"* in *Rites of Passage*.

When Paul falls off his horse (before he becomes specifically religious), he has not been personally suffering, but he has been watching Christians being slaughtered too many times, and he "snaps". He can't take it anymore and falls off his horse.

Have you ever "fallen off your horse"? If so, you get a feeling for how *Rites of Passage* begin, religious or otherwise. Sometimes they happen once in Life, and sometimes far more often.

They usually occur in three stages according to Turner: (1) *Separation or* Alienation from existing rules and regulations, then (2) the *Liminal* or *Threshold* stage of strange new experiences and understandings, leading to (3) the *Incorporation (literally Embodiment)* of a new and more socially oriented role in society.

Thus Turner was involved as an Anthropologist in descriptions of Performance Stages in the Transformations of Cultures. So we have passed through the *Alienation* stage of the early 20th century, are now wandering about in the *Liminality* Stage, and Hope to Cope in an integrated *Communitas* not only individually but collectively.

The following story illustrates both an individual and cultural model at the same time. Again I am keeping this on a general level. It may sound, however, like a very slow moving "testimony" at the black church in *Blues Brothers*, where "the light shines".

My personal *Transmogrification* (dictionary definition: transformation in a magical or surprising manner), has taken over 30 years and is continuing. Its 3 stages resemble for me the 3 Categories of Peirce and John, *and* Rites of Passage as *Performances* described by Turner.

You may think that I am not only a slow learner or even worse, have learned nothing. Let's see, OK?

The First Stage of my Transmogrification: I see my young son die and I "snap" and "fall off my horse". My son dies approaching one year old, after we are told that if the original diagnosis of Leukemia at his birth is true, he's the first human ever to die as a result of being born with it, which doctors thought *extremely* unlikely. He is a bright, happy child for months, but as he nears his first birthday, his energy suddenly begins draining away, and in a few weeks he dies with his baby-blue eyes staring into mine.

I am already in the midst of my grad studies. Established religion seems distant and detached. I turn to a study of Primal Rituals, but I find nothing like that around me. My last effort at traditional religion is the graduate seminar on Religion and Art of Europe mentioned earlier.

At the Orvieto Cathedral in northern Italy, I sit transfixed before Signorelli's *The Resurrection of the Body*, a copy of which is today above one of doors of my study. The painting, four centuries before Salvador Dali, shows scores of deceased humans emerging from a solid white plain in various stages, from skeletal to embodied resuscitation.

Soon after that we get to Basel, Switzerland, and one afternoon I visit the famous theologian Karl Barth in his home. He is in his mid-80s and despite his reputation as a fierce iconoclast, he is delightful in conversation. We don't actually talk much about theology. We talk mainly about Mozart. I tell him of my performance while in college as Figaro in *The Marriage of Figaro* with a violin section from New York in our orchestra, and off we go. We both love Mozart.

I do mention my experience at the Orvieto Cathedral, but I realize while describing it that I am already speaking a different kind of language from his Top-Down theology that always *begins* with God, that Revelation is not only surprising but always involves God. My version of the Signorelli Bodily Resurrection *was* and *is* more **Bottom-Up** as the beginning of my *Embodiment*. (I am not saying all Top-Down thinking is bad. More about that in Part 4, Scene 5.)

By the time I get back to Northwestern, I realize that I'm an Atheist, and strange as it may seem, I still consider Atheism the *first stage* of my "more or less religious" Transmogrification, and in keeping with the first stage of dramatic changes that Turner calls *Alienation*.

When I describe my atheistic intentions to Richard Ellmann, the great Joyce scholar, he doesn't try to dissuade me but suggests I take enough time to feel sure of this. Edmund Perry, chair of the religion department says don't worry, he'd be glad to hire an atheist in his department after a few years elsewhere, the usual procedure for Ph.D. grads. Perhaps I should have taken him up on this, but never did, and he died several years ago.

The Second Stage takes place during my first teaching position at the new state college in Michigan I described earlier, during which the *Dionysius in 69* experience reported earlier occurred. During two sabbaticals, I become credentialed as a Gestalt therapist at the Gestalt Institute of Cleveland under Irving and Miriam Polster, the leading trainers in the country since Fritz Perls originated it.

There I dealt with not only my son's death but mine *as* a child when I became a "serious-minded" adult, i.e., I experienced a return to my *childhood* Embodiment.

Thus the Second Stage of my Transmogrification *blossoms* as I discover the *Child Within Me* that I left behind in the pig-wallow. When Miriam Polster says to me along the way: "Jesse, you are such a little boy in a such a big body", the little boy from the pig-wallow thinks he is ready to fly.

Stage 2 according to Turner, however, is still often chaotic and unstable. What looked like a great a job offer in California at the Gestalt Institute of San Diego was like a Canadian goose landing in snapping turtles. I should have looked more carefully where I was landing.

It was nothing like the Gestalt Institute in Cleveland. What looked like lots of referrals was hardly any with few possibilities of getting more. In desperation I land part-time teaching at SDSU.

I also begin attending services at the San Diego Church of Religious Science, where Terry Cole Whittaker of Religious Science fame drawing over a thousand every Sunday morning. Perhaps she needs a new counseling service there. She eventually did with guess who?

The Third Stage of my Transmogrification begins here, the stage of Incorporation. I attend a social meeting connected with the church and meet my "luscious lump of feminine pulchritude" second wife Bonnie, and the swirl of a new kind of Affordance reaches into my ongoing efforts to develop my Survival Strategies.

However, she has four children and is going through certain bankruptcy due to her alcoholic first husband's business failure. To top this off, her youngest child has a very low IQ of 57. My older four daughters were already on their way into the brave new world.

How can the love of two such Fragile Lovers succeed? Yet we somehow rise together above our circumstances. As we fall madly in love, an old mid-western song that comes to mind: "Glow little glow worm. Glimmer, glimmer." We glimmered together, and many months later I finally manage to settle into a new practice in the Scripps Hospital complex.

Her famous line has always been: "Jesse do you *feel* it?" My answer is always, "Yes, Yes," until years into our marriage, I exclaim to her that I finally figured out what is "it" in "Do you feel it?" It is "us". She's held me closer ever since, through thick and thin, including the illness that eventually kills her 30 years into our marriage. That makes us *soul-mates*, right? *This personal merging with her is the beginning of my third stage of Transmogrification.*

I also realize early in our relationship that she has something within her that I do not. She always seems to feel at home and *belong* wherever she is. She loves everybody and almost everybody seems to love her. Whatever I achieved in my first two stages, I realize that nobody in their right mind would describe me that way. *I strongly disliked lots of people and even hated some*. So the enthusiastic child within me since my second stage was still missing something.

This is when I coincidentally begin to read C. S. Peirce, and influences begin to coalesce. Peirce finds love in three different levels of evolution: (1) the Emergence of living things from no-thingness, (2) the inter-connective level where things begin to make sense inside and out, and (3) as Peirce (and the Gospel of John) would put it, the blossoming of *Love* as an alternative to the inevitable decay that results in what Peirce calls *Destiny*. Sounds like Turner, too, doesn't it?

The only way that most animals deal with this is in the propagation and allegiance with its kin. We often follow that model, too. At any rate we *Participate* (thanks again Arnold) in our culture and surroundings. And on top of all that, both Bonnie and I love old Corvettes.

But, thus far I have said nothing about God, although I do have four big paintings above the bookshelves of my study: (1) A painting from Bali two friends sent to me of a tribal ceremony about to start, (2) Signorelli's *The Resurrection of the Body*, (3) the bizarre cubic style painting by Picasso of the *Crucifixion* he never wanted to sell despite his being an atheist, and recently (4) Leonardo Da Vinci's famous painting of Jesus looking us in the eye, the original of which recently sold for 450 million dollars.

About the Picasso painting, Picasso's widow insisted that the painting is more Catholic than the Pope. The subject is the cross, with Christ's now dead and Mary Magdalene's still anguishing body is draped over his, both bodies in silvery white. In bright colors his sorrowful mother is to the far right side. Closer to Jesus' cross are other victims, a horsed soldier with a spear, another on a ladder climbing up to take Jesus down, others gambling for clothes.

Except for the Bali painting, you can find the other 3 paintings easily on the internet. For the Bali painting that I also described earlier, I can send you a copy.

In the last few months of Bonnie's life, the pain from her strange neurological illness was unaffected even by Morphine. Her pain became so great that she could no longer allow me to hold her in my arms. I could only hold her hand.

However, when I ask her just before the end whether she still loves me, the pain suddenly seems to disappear and I am able to hold her in my arms as she smiles while saying her last words: "Jesse, I don't just love you, I adore you." I am exaggerating nothing. This is no movie.

Her influence continues. In the 30 years of our marriage and 10 years since her "apparent" death (recall Bond's comment about M (as played by Judy Dent) in an early passage in *Spectre*. Bonnie like M has never let death get in her way.

About God, more about that in Part 4, Scene 5.

PART 4

APPLICATIONS IN EMBODIED LIFE
THE EDGE OF TOMORROW

In the middle of the night recently I suddenly awake as something "dawns on me" out of the blue: the numbers 7 and 1917 and the names Tunney and Dempsey. At first I thought of Humpty and Dumpty, about whom I had written lately, but after racking my brain a while recalled my father telling me when I was a child of a great boxing match between Jack Dempsey and Gene Tunney, so I looked it up on-line.

It was in 1917 when Dempsey flattened Tunney in the 7th round, but standing gloriously over him, refused to return to his corner while the ref counted to 10 over Tunney during his famous "slow count", which was so slow it allowed Tunney to get back up on his feet again. Tunney eventually won the fight not by a knock-out but by points. (You can look this up online if you like.)

Why on Earth would I have this "vision" while thinking about Part 4? Then I recalled Nassim Taleb's comments about "partial successes" and "partial failures". Dempsey and Tunney were both great illustrations of both at the same time in the same fight.

Then I realized how I had knocked myself out trying to think of a movie for Part 4. In every one I considered, I either didn't like the movie or the actors and actresses in it.

The closest I came for a movie was *The Edge of Tomorrow* where Tom Cruise and his colleague Rita (Emily Blunt) are in gory battle after battle with grotesque extraterrestrial aliens who are trying to conquer the Earth and appear to be winning.

After many literally Life and Death episodes where they die and surprisingly find themselves alive again back where they were earlier, the movie continues.

This movie was made in 2014, so you have had plenty of time to see it, but if you have not but might after what is described above, and *don't* like *spoilers*, skip over the rest of this Part 4 Intro section and go to Part 4 Scene 1. The movie won't be mentioned again before that.

Finally after many such events, they and their support team are facing the alien chief monster, realizing it will really be not only their last battle in the war but that this time they have no chance to come back to life again.

This time it is a suicide mission for sure, because they will not just die of bullet wounds. They have to blow up the entire territory, including themselves, *but* the Destruction won't stop unless they save the world. Tom even convinces his small support team to go with them into this last battle.

Where I come from, this is called *Going For the Gizzard*. As they prepare for this confrontation, Tom and Rita converse about the fact that this is sure death for them, and he simply turns to her and says: "We have seen worse".

They do in fact both die as martyrs in far more grueling circumstances than they have ever had before, ending with Tom's planting the suicide bomb right in the face of the extraterrestrial monster. It goes off with an enormous KABOOM, and the monster and both he and Rita are blown to tiny bits.

Then Tom to his super-surprise finds himself alive again, having obviously by his uniform been promoted from Major to Colonel and on a plane on its way to an enormous celebration that the war is now over at the military center where the movie begins. He passes a building with a huge panel showing Rita as the "Angel of Verdun".

He wanders through the facility and passes all their support team somehow marching again, and turns down the passageway where he first met Rita at the beginning of the movie while doing her military exercise prone on the floor.

She is again in the same place doing the same exercise. When she sees him approaching, she raises up, turns toward him, seeming to have no idea who he is, and says the same thing she has said before: "What do you want?"

The movie closes with him smiling at her.

I suppose there are several reasons why I would chose this movie but didn't (more or less) to start Part 4. It certainly raises the question of where Partial Successes and Failures can possibly go. Will there ever be an end to our need for Survival Strategies? At this moment I haven't the foggiest, other than the plain fact that *The Edge of Tomorrow* is now one of my favorite movies.

So let's continue where we left off at the end of Part 3 with another round of the same 5 Cultural Survival Strategies: Art, Ethics, Science, Politics, and Religion.

PART 4
SCENE 1 ARTISTIC APPLICATIONS: THE PREGNANCY OF ART

Many years ago soon after I moved to Michigan, as I briefly reported earlier, my colleague Carolyn Thomas and her husband Timothy, who taught at a local college, saved enough money to take a year-long trip around the world, so I sent money with them for artwork from Bali.

They sent inside a big bamboo rod a Bali painting hat is about 4 feet wide and 3 feet high. It provides some information about Life in Primal Bali, but it is how it *Feels* that it Affect/Effects you. If you would like a copy, if you write to you1@verizon.net, I will send you one.

In short, surrounding the small village and its buildings are large "tree bathing" trees that provide a setting for tribal members approaching the village on a solid green plain with drums, instruments, and food for a ritual likely to involve drum beats, chants, dances, and music that will encourage ecstatic states reminiscent of primal human rituals. In those days art and religion were virtually the same thing.

In time, however, Art and Religion begin to pull apart, as described earlier, resulting in the Secular side of Arts and everything else today.

Nevertheless, as you know, in the movie *Blues Brothers*, secularized John Belushi and Dan Aykroid enter a black Church and a glowing light draws them into the *ecstatic* dancing with parishioners. Add to this the pre-Christian *Dionysius in 69* and the *Who* concert at Fillmore East, and we have moments when Art and Religion seem to come together again.

By and large, however, the smooth relation of this Humpty (Art) and Dumpty (Religion) has gone off the wall. Can they be put back tougher again? See what you think by the time we reach Part 4, Scene 5.

During my interdepartmental Ph.D. program at Northwestern, in the philosophy department I learned a great deal from Professor James Edie, an expert in Maurice Merleau-Ponty, whose *Phenomenology of Perception* revolutionized what in the title of this book is called *Making Sense of Things*.

In short, he negates the prominence of *passive* and *objective/mechanical* interpretations of Stimulus-Response Reactions (as when stuck with a pin) in favor of an *active* and *lively* way of *Making Sense* of things right down to the very bottom of Perception itself. So Perception is not just something being written down on a chalk board. Our Active Minds are *doing* the writing.

To me this means Education is more a matter of learning to Make Sense of things than learning what we are told Objectively. Charter Schools are usually more likely than Public Schools to teach this way.

My first teaching job after receiving my Ph.D. was at the brand-new Saginaw Valley College (later State University) in Michigan just down the road from the National Headquarters of Dow Chemical.

There I developed our Environmental Learning Program in a large classroom with wrap-around screens and a carpeted floor with big pillows so students could move around *in* what they were learning rather than learn *about* things in the traditional way.

I helped recruit two new faculty members, one of whom Curt McCray went on to become President of Long Beach State University here in California for several years. During 10 years at now SVSU I received two sabbatical leaves at the Gestalt Institute of Cleveland (best training school in Gestalt Therapy in the country) and earned post-grad certification as a Gestalt Therapist.

I since then "migrated" to practice at the Gestalt Institute of San Diego, adjunct teaching at San Diego State University, a practice first in downtown La Jolla, then the Scripps Hospital Complex, etc. Through all of this I focused on bringing together the relation of Perception and Reflection together in every way possible.

Meanwhile Merleau-Ponty had died when only 53 years old from a sudden heart attack, and his unfinished *Nature* lectures at the Sorbonne and his book *Visible and Invisible* were eventually published just as he left them. *In both books he moves from Perception to its Sources in what philosophers call Being.*

Here is his new twist. He discards not only the claims of Renaissance Rationality to replace the Cosmic Hierarchy of Platonic Age with its own Cosmic Hierarchy of Being, he sought to replace both Platonic and Renaissance interpretations of this. *Being is found Between feeling and thought, "not abstractly beyond them Up-There Somewhere Else".*

For Merleau-Ponty *Being* is Here. You walk around in it every day, and you don't have to die in order to live in it. *Being is Life itself as it Evolves.* It is an Alive, not a Dead stimulus-response kind of thing. At least this is my understanding of him. He was deeply influenced by both Gestalt Psychology and Phenomenology.

So why all this introduction in order to describe Art? It all begins to shape up early in the 20th century first when the Gestalt psychologist Wolfgang Kohler, and much later Jean Piaget in his *A Child's Conception of Causality*, argue that a child's *Spontaneous Experience* rather than *Objective Thought* is their original way of understanding things.

In short, children *Sense* things *directly* rather than think *about* them, so they *Sense* what will happen next without thinking *about* it. So Kohler and Piaget are consistent with what Damasio describes as Ultra-Instinctive Survival Strategies, which begin in our neurological system.

We might go even deeper than this. Children carry within them what might be called the *Maternal Bond*. Instead of seeing *distinctions* between this and that, this and that are *bonded*, as is a mother and child, even after the child is born. So children see not just what distinguishes things but what *Bonds* them.

A single sentence to summarize the last two paragraphs: *Children are the Embodiment of Ultra-Sensitive Survival Strategies, that bond things together emotionally. Schools need to be careful therefore not to crush these roots that all too easily penetrate into Life itself with too many Rootless and Disembodied details.*

Objective thought can provide a supplement for a child's way of thinking, but learning through Spontaneous Experience and the *Feel* of things needs *not* go away as its foundation for experiencing Cause and Effect, which otherwise becomes lost in mechanical ways of understanding things. In effect, Children are often sterilized by standard education not only in *what* to think but *how*.

This is where Art comes in: Artists (as grown-up children) who have not forgotten how important Sensitive Experience continues in Life, as in either children or any of us when we *Experience* an Artist's work. The question is not what you think *About* it but how it *Feels spontaneously*.

Now back to Merleau-Ponty to illustrate this. He speaks for example of how early 20th century painters describe the Depth of objects by using *colors* to describe that *depth* in a way that cameras cannot, so you can *feel* that depth by looking at that art in a way that takes you *Inside* it. Consider the *colors*, not just the *object boundaries* as in Cubist art for example.

Have you ever looked at children's art. They are already beginning to experience things this way. Unfortunately, again, education is often good at ruining children, but Fortunately not always, because they do still offer classes in the Arts.

Merleau-Ponty's post-dualistic thinking focuses on Lived Experience and its Embedded Relationships, discovering the *Immanent Presence* of things behind their "sensuous surface". That is the way both children and artists usually experience things.

It's also how phenomenologists begin their investigations with what is called *Phenomenological Reduction*, where the first step is "suspending" all *objective* presuppositions, no matter what they are. It is "scientific" in that in the spontaneous process that ensues, not by numbers but whether its results agree with anyone else who uses the same kind of procedures.

Perhaps this description will help those who are neither children nor artists to understand what is at stake here. Children and Artists won't usually need this introduction.

Back to Merleau-Ponty, his approach is different from human ideas and scientific theories as we *usually* understand them. For him Art is a Medium that allows the depths of Experience to come to the surface with *Extreme Attentiveness*.

"Deconstruction" is a popular investigation process today. In this case, however, there is no *construction* to *deconstruct*. Art reaches beneath understanding constructions as *objective* ways.

For Merleau-Ponty, *Perceptual Pregnancy* as a summary of what has been said to this point and is derived from the descent of Perception from Visible to Invisible by way of Empirical Gestalts (experiential formulations). *Art definitely qualifies as Pregnant.*

Notice how often his phrases sound like Pregnancy: "a power to break forth", "productivity", "poses itself by its own means", "not as a 'consciousness' but an *inhabitant* of the body", "beyond the objective body as a painting is beyond the canvas", etc.

If such terms fit Art generally, they certainly fit Music, the primary focus in Part 3, Scene 1. Merleau-Ponty usually focuses on artistic *space* rather than *time*. When he speaks of music, he speaks of things like the way a musician becomes one with his or her instrument.

Music, too, fits the Pregnant phrases above, not only in the artist, but in those who Participate in the art as viewer or listener, as in the cartoon of the fellow entering and exiting a Picasso Exhibit. For Merleau-Ponty the arts generally Affect/Effect our experience rather than merely provide *objective interpretations*.

My mother was a musician, and her music definitely affected her body and her behavior as well as mine. My father, not a musician by any stretch, nevertheless spontaneously *hummed* little tunes to himself everywhere he went, while he drove his car, shopped, or whatever. Even when everyone else was singing at church, he hummed. I am sure he hummed while I was being born.

When it comes right down to it, don't most of us do something similar, whistle while we work, tap our fingers on the steering wheel while we drive, etc. Music moves us in one way or another, perhaps not as wildly as in a primal ritual like the one that begins this Scene, nor the church parishioners in Blues Brothers, but we at least echo them, right?

Art is a very visceral thing, including causing riots when the French audience reportedly first heard Stravinsky's *Rite of Spring* or saw Picasso's paintings. To put it in Merleau-Ponty's way, all of Art, wherever it is found, arises from Pregnant Space and Silence.

PART 4
SCENE 2 ETHICAL APPLICATIONS: CHILDHOOD ETHICS

In the TV series *The Young Pope* the (fictitious) Young Pope at the end of the 10th and final episode is addressing a large gathering of the faithful in front of a famous cathedral in which he recalls a story of young Saint Juana, who died at the age of 18.

A group of pre-adolescent children ask her questions that pre-adolescent children today might ask. I have rearranged them a bit, but they include:

Am I true or am I false?

Am I dead or am I alive?

Am I sick or am I well?

Am I good or am I bad?

Am I clean or am I dirty?

Am I a fool or am I smart?

Am I young or am I old?

Am I woman or am I man?

Am I warm or am I cold?

Am I king or am I servant?

Am I rich or am I poor?

Am I happy or am I sad?

Am I lost or am I found?

Do I have time or has it run out?

As a pre-adolescent child and even since then at one time or another I have asked them all. How about you?

The rest of this Scene will consider how such questions arise in the first place and how they lead to Ethics as we grow up as embodied humans.

Julia Kristeva, a Bulgarian-French psychoanalyst and humanist, is the author of a book you will find in Recommended Books, *The Incredible Need to Believe*. The title makes it sound like she is a very religious person, which is not the case. She considers herself as *Pre-Religious*, meaning she identifies with Humanism, not Religion as such.

Religion is far too objectivist to suit her, although she thinks religion was on a valid path until it became too doctrinal and ritualistic. So for her personally Humanism is Pre-Religious (although historically Humanism emerged *following* the Renaissance and is not all that anti-doctrinal). In any case she also says at times her Humanism is Post-Christian.

She nevertheless enjoys her conversations with religious thinkers like Richard Kearney, who describes himself as one of several "Anatheists", who believe in God but in such a way that the definition of God needs dramatic revision. In Kearney's book *Reimaging the Sacred*, he interviews Kristeva. What is it that distinguishes them from the Objectivists they Object to?

I have sympathies for both Humanism and Anatheism, but I identify with neither, as you probably assume from Scene 5 in both Parts 3 and 4. However, I believe she is on the right path concerning how Ethics do emerge in childhood, although Pragmatists, Gestalt Psychologists, and Phenomenologists agree with many of her Psychoanalyst notions about childhood.

Kristeva, however, describes childhood in clearer Ethical detail than anyone else, so the next several paragraphs follow her path with a few comments along the way.

Kristeva is concerned today especially because of the chaotic condition of Adolescents. At the time of her interview with Richard Kearney, there were nearly 2 million French adolescents who were NEET (Neither Employed nor in Education or Training). She holds that they are still what she calls *"Believers"* since childhood, but their "believing" has become notoriously chaotic. *What does she mean by "Believing"?*

She begins with the inherent Singularity described earlier in this book. *Every child is spontaneously Unique*, and the uniqueness develops in a way similar not only to Sigmund Freud but other thinkers like William James, Kohler, Piaget, and Merleau-Ponty.

However, She alone concentrates well on the problems of today's Adolescents in their warped early childhood. Adolescents still have a version of sorts of early childhood love for parents, but Desire for them has turned to *Sadomasochism and* either self-punishment (Masochism) or destructive behavior (which she calls "Kamikaze Syndrome"). In either case the result is *Adolescent Nihilism*. How did this start in early childhood?

The earliest childhood contact is with Mother, the earliest and most intimate sensory contact with the surrounding world, and *Absolute Certainty of Security and Satisfaction*, beginning with mother and then father, although hardly any of us remember those days today. They are Primal Emotional Processes.

With both mother and father we have someone to whom we can Listen and who Listens to us, so we can persist in speaking, and we get Credit for what we say and also get Credit for what we do, which is where Ethics enters the Scene.

In short, our early contacts with our surroundings lead us to Believe In our parents, ourselves, and develop emotionally our way of Making Sense of and Doing things. The basic orientation therefore is not What to Believe but where to find Belief as Confidence in Living.

As this kind of *Belief* continues, however, parental identification can of course be idealized into God as our imaginary father when father is not present, which to Freud is Regressive Archaism. That is certainly one way to look at it.

The basic problem therefore occurs when Primal Belief changes from *Who to "Believe In" into "What to Believe" and the basic emotional grounding is lost.* Everyone and/or Everything around us however and not just "God" may be telling us *What to Believe and What to Do.* Meanwhile *Who is in then trustable, if anyone, for either children or adolescents? Today's chaotic surroundings are not helping much.*

Believability and Belief shifts as we grow up from parents (supposing that they were there for us), to teachers (in my case my family and neighboring farmers, later teachers like Mr. Hildebrand), and whoever else can be *Believed In*. The older we get, the more everything is up for grabs. *The test in any case is not basically What to Believe Objectively but How to have Confidence In either ourselves or those around us.*

Belief as Creed, (Credo) for Kristeva is a term that goes all the way back to Sanskrit writing, meaning "to give ones heart, one's *vital force*, in the expectation of a reward". *This is not therefore a Legalistic or Objective matter, but one of the Heart. It is again an "Act of Confidence".* In Christian history she acknowledges that Augustine was the first "to read the Scripture with the eyes and heart fixed upon our heart".

Admittedly, when human parentage is projected into God, what Freud calls Regressive Archaism can appear, as it can with or without God, in plain language transforming *Living Issues* into *Dead Ends* with Nowhere to go. Sound familiar?

As a child I was taught a standard night-time prayer that included: "If I should die before I wake, I pray the Lord my soul to take." Did you ever pray that as a child? It is a prayer that focuses on Fear and Guilt, asking our Heavenly Father for help, which to me then meant to make it through the night without dying and going to Hell.

Back to parents for a moment, child-raising can actually be a learning experience for both parents and children. As a child I recall my mother once refusing to allow me another of her home-made cookies, to which I said "Damn, Shit", imitating older students on the school bus when frustrated. My father then came over to me and said: "What did you call your mother?" and I said "I didn't call her anything".

He decked me with a slap on the face, and he and my mother walked out of the room. My mother came back later and said: "You need to know that your father is out on the front porch crying because he struck his son." To put it briefly, he never struck me again but we talked a lot more when there were problems, and I never used profanity with my mother again. I admit, however, that the church we attended resembled Freud's evaluation, as many do.

Kristeva calls "oceanic feeling" the ultimate result of continuing what we start in early childhood and reaches the *Unnamable*, which mobilizes experientially an extreme intensity of the five senses, where she claims Humanist metaphors will help far more than objective thoughts. Again I admit that I learned most of that at home and in the woods.

This also resembles what Merleau-Ponty calls the *Unnamable Sources* of all our language. More about that in Scene 5. What he calls *Elementals*, however, are far more than metaphors. For understandable reasons perhaps, I am going off course here.

But for me this raises the problems of how Quantum theory in Science and Gestalt theory in early 20th century are a strange kind of what Stuart Kaufman calls *Adjacent Possibles*, which appear similar without any causality explanation either inside themselves or together have some *enchanting* similarity.

Perhaps a clear explanation will be found someday, but it is another of those things that have not happened so far and may never be. However, it does provide a different description of God from Freud's explanation of God as an Objective projection.

We will come back to all this in Scene 5. For now let's return to the problems of children and adolescents.

In any case, I agree with Kristeva when she puts it beautifully that children grow up "not yet oneself" and are too often swallowed up in today's "not-yet world." No wonder children become so confused ethically today. It is very confusing for not only adolescents but adults who can be *Believed In*, let alone *What to Believe Objectively*.

As a last note concerning *The Young Pope*, near the conclusion of his address he looks out and sees his parents, who had abandoned him as a child. When at the end of his address he asks the gathering to smile, his parents do not smile. They leave.

Our culture, including the Church, has a lot to learn concerning how to raise our children. How many of us who are parents, teachers, or other "elders" can smile and our children will smile back?

PART 4
SCENE 3 SCIENCE APPLICATIONS: NATURE AND ANIMALS AS SCIENTISTS

It "dawned on me" one day that Nature itself was the first and perhaps greatest of all scientists because our entire history is an evolutionary process at work, which is how C.S. Peirce described it over a century ago.

Nature today is certainly not where it was over 13.8 billion years ago. Why? Because Scientific Nature has been at work. That is surely one way to look at it given in our age of complex systems.

Especially when considering Self-Motivating Agents in Dynamic Complex Systems, whether inanimate or animate, they make dramatic changes in things that then repeat and confirm their Changes until new and different Experiments occur.

So you don't even have to be human to be a Scientist in this Sense, because if you blend my last part of the book into this one, Science is full of scientists whether animals or Nature itself, which was doing things scientifically in every complex ways before animals appear on Earth and continue that job themselves. Human scientists simply imitate such procedures in developing what today we call Scientific Method.

Along Evolution's Path organic life appears, and *all* such Life presents Living Evolutionary models. Even *Plants* illustrate Scientific Method at Work.

Although my old friend the Paramecium's have not done much that is different over the eons that they have been here, another single-celled creature, the Amoeba has apparently *learned* somehow to trap a paramecium for a meal. Granted that it may originally have been simply a lucky accident that led them eventually to make a habit of this, but then scientists today often use that variation on scientific method too, don't they?

After all, scientists too discover many accidental successes, although that does not show on official listings of Scientific Method, which usually goes like this:

Make an observation.

Ask a question.

Form a hypothesis, with a predictable and testable explanation.

Test the prediction.

Iterate (Repeat) results to confirm the hypothesis and prove the reliability of such predictions. (Of course that may involve lucky accidents along the way.)

If you subtract self-consciousness and reflective thinking, Nature often seems to do the same kinds of thing, and complex pre-human animals have a consciousness of sorts although rarely self-consciousness, and yet produce amazing products without so far as we know even thinking about it. Recall some of their extremely Complex Products described earlier. Doesn't this make human scientists occasionally seem like "Junior G-Men of the Air"?

This is how Nature and Animals got where they are today compared to where they were a few thousand years ago, and this includes us humans, which is quite impressive, right?

Scientists do improve on Nature's experiments of course by adding self-consciousness. In any event, Nature has been quite successful scientifically in its own way however for billions of years. It has its accomplishments and Science has theirs. We have to admit, however, that we are a wonderful accomplishment of theirs, agreed?

Nature stands therefore alongside Science for success stories, even "acknowledging" we are much more versatile in many ways than other animals with our billions upon billions of neurons and our mobile appendages, both in-board and out-board.

We have certainly moved way beyond chimps who according to recent research are just unable to understand words, let alone language. Chimps do use rocks to crack nuts, and Raccoons use rocks to crack eggs. I don't know enough to speak for Chimps, but Raccoons have demonstrated to me that they can parent Special children, pigs have learned how to use mud as a good sun protector, etc. Animal learning in how to develop Survival Strategies is indeed impressive.

However, I admit that we humans are to be sure far more Creative and Efficient in designing tools of intricate types. I don't know any animals who can develop either Sub-Atomic Particle Theories or Deep Space Astronomical Theories. However it was Nature that (or who) developed both sub-atomic particles and deep space realities.

But let's shift the issue to *self-improvement*. Scientists have created cures for many diseases, as in my father's instrumentation of Penicillin from chicken eggs many years ago. Today fascinating work is being done with Gene Studies, etc.

But consider whether we have improved us all that much in our Behavior. We still have much less successful travel statistics than bats, right?

Consider how young fauns have learned how to protect themselves with on-board white spots and then discard them as they grow up and fend for themselves. Consider the on-board tools of Australian Cuttlefish, who have learned how in a few seconds to make themselves invisible as a *disguise* device when threatened and in another few seconds very conspicuous as an *attractor* device. You can go online to see for yourself Cuttlefish Camouflage techniques. It is impressive. How did they learn do this, purely accidentally?

Any scientist who could develop this ability for us humans would deserve several Nobel Prizes. The best we can do as humans so far like that is to *Repel* threats with very out-board weaponry or by a calling the police.

To *Attract* outboard attention, we have to buy very expensive clothes. Inboard, all we can do depends on how good looking we are, especially as we take off some (or all) of our clothes. However, no matter how attractive we make ourselves, we won't for that get any Nobel Prizes.

Nor will we get Nobel Prizes for our tattoos, which can be either *attractor* or *repeller*, depending on who is looking at them and/or where they are located on the body. Besides, we cannot Embody or Erase our in-board tools spontaneously the way cuttlefish can.

In their skin and elsewhere animals *Learn new things*. Granted however long it takes to develop experientially and experimentally how to develop their Survival Coping Strategies, *they can do it*.

Thus we develop our human strategies, adding our reflective abilities to those of our animal predecessors, although without our reflective abilities animals demonstrate many impressive lessons that work quite well Pragmatically, which is their natural way of Doing things.

So let's face it. In our Scientific Methods we are imitating Nature and its Animals, both of which have been doing such things for ages.

To be sure, Science moves a lot *faster* than Nature. Look what Scientists have done in the last century. A century is a very small drop in the very large bucket for Nature, so Nature has all the time it wants, which is more than we can say for us.

In a single lifetime for us humans, we have many big-time products to show for it, such as computers and other electronic devices, etc. So there are obviously advantages in Science, *as long as* scientists gear themselves *in the same direction* as Evolution does, focusing on Survival Strategies generally and for us humans in such a way that we all Live Together happily. Grant that Environmental Science at its best may do this, but even its record is not Lilly white.

All Science of whatever type revolves around *Life*. And as described near the end of Part 3, Scene 3, Albert Schweitzer's *Reverence for Life is at the root of all Science*. I've tried hard to remind scientists about this.

This raises questions about whether animals or scientists measure up well to Schweitzer's standard. Both Scientists and Animals both score well and sometimes poorly. In animals, Mothers certainly score much higher than fathers if you recall Momma Raccoon on one side and on the other the Lion King who kills his own children. Far worse than that, Nature has created Hurricanes and Plagues, not to mention Tornados if you recall my personal experience with one. Nature can also hit us with a large meteor.

Then again, we have Scientists who create terrible Nuclear Weapons. Ask the Japanese about this. Even worse, various products of science that were meant well at first are now capable of killing extensive plant, animal, and human life.

Don't get me wrong. As I have said elsewhere, I love my computer and Bose system. Far more important, Dr. Romero at UCSD Medical Center several yeas ago saved my life, intelligence, and sanity, so who am I to complain about Science?

Besides, as a practicing psychologist for many years, I may not be a laboratory scientist but am a member of The American Association for the Advancement of Science and subscribe to its elaborate journal *Science*, which I read regularly. Despite what I have said, I confess that I love Science for what it has accomplished.

So I am not advocating a simple and science-free Amish-style society, *but* we really do need to give Nature and its Creatures credit alongside Science for putting us where we are today. So please agree that Nature and its Animal Scientists set a pretty good stage on which Human Scientists can perform. Would you acknowledge at least that much? *After all, it was Nature that invented Life, including You and me.*

PART 4
SCENE 4 POLITICAL APPLICATIONS:
POLITICAL SURVIVAL IN THE 21ST CENTURY

Part 4, Scene 4 picks up where Part 3, Scene 4 and Part 4, Scene 2 leave off. Let's start with Education today and what needs to be done Politically.

Consider the issue of Charter Schools (and School Choice), where statistics clearly show better grades on standard tests than public schools in the same area. The Body Politic has made it clear that more Charter Schools are needed. Token gestures are not enough for the long waiting lines of parents who have become more *Engaged* in their children's, especially black children's, access to Charter Schools. I'm very proud of those parents for their persistence.

However, Labor Unions oppose this since they and the Democratic Far Left Wing would rather "defend" inept public school teachers and the Power of Unions rather than the best Education for students. They promote nasty demonstrations against the Secretary of Education everywhere she makes appeals for Charter Schools.

Actually, they really seem to want more Union members and radical Democrat votes, hoping Biden (who currently seemed at first to stand for moderate programs to be migrating toward far left wing) will close down Charter schools, which will establish union control of *all* public education.

If Biden does that, there will likely be protests by Black parents that will disgrace him, since over a million families are now in line for Charter schools. Perhaps he will see his foolishness and migrate back toward more moderate Democrat voters.

Who again is being *served* here politically? The *served* are certainly not the students. Ask black parents who want better education for their children.

Unfortunately, Unions are not always what they used to be. Like Political Parties, they too often have often become Top-Heavy, Disembodied, and Rigid (Ideological), mainly interested in their own Power. Is it any wonder that workers in a new car manufacturing plant recently voted down union membership by a 2-1 average. Some unions need to change their ways.

But rather than see this as just another polarized issue, there are perhaps middle ground options that will not satisfy union leaders but satisfy *some* teachers and virtually *all* parents and students.

Among such options are (1), Limiting union officer terms in office, (2) retraining some public school teachers in new methods successfully tested in Charter schools, (3) making retirement more desirable for inept teachers (who might really like to retire if they could afford it), (4) allowing Charter Schools to have even more access to empty public school classrooms, (5) setting up more public school experiments imitating and/or even improving Charter methods, etc.

Unfortunately it is not all that simple, especially in huge cities. The new *absolutely unchallengeable claims about Charter Schools and Their Enemies* just became published by Thomas Sowell of Stanford University.

It includes extremely detailed studies of both Charter and Local City Schools in the Same Neighborhoods with the Same Number of Students, Racial Percentages, Economic States, Size of Family, etc. This research consistently shows superior results in Charter schools.

Then *why* are there 50,000 mostly black students who are on the waiting lines for admission to Charter schools just in New York and over a million in this country? The answer is very simple: Politicians and Union Leaders.

They are "resisting" not only the formation of bigger or more Charter schools but closing them down despite their success. They are already demanding how existing Charter schools teach such things as "sex education" and "ethnic studies". Even worse they are rewriting school history books with leftist political biases in order to brainwash students. Shouldn't *Parents* have a bigger place in how or what their children are learning in such courses?

If you are such a parent with young children, no matter what you racial background, you *owe* it to your children to read Thomas Sowell's book. He is a very famous scholar who also happens to be black, and is speaking for all racial backgrounds.

Sometimes civil and political Disagreements continue back and forth forever, but sometimes there are options in which everyone is more satisfied rather than be constantly frustrated and upset. Sometimes that never occurs.

Consider the Harvard president's reaction to C.S. Peirce as a young man who "smarted off" about him over a century ago, as described earlier. Harvard University Press finally published their classic collection of C. S. Peirce's Works three decades after Peirce's death, and that may have made that president roll over in his grave, but it could have occurred while Peirce was still alive, right?

Peirce's life as America's Greatest Thinker who Created Pragmatism, etc. ended in poverty, all because the Harvard President's *Revenge*, which today of course would politely be called *Obstruction* or *Resistance*.

Consider Signorelli's fresco in the Orvieto Cathedral where those Risen from the Dead are talking with each other. I am surprised that they were not dancing since the Angels above them are sounding their horns.

However, what do you suppose the Risen Dead are talking with each other *about*? I doubt it was how to start a new war between

Catholics and Protestants, or even how to find a golf course for only Democrats or Republicans. After all, this is supposedly a place beyond that kind of thing.

In my adolescence I am in a wrestling match with a young bull friend of mine, which I had always won before, but now he is growing up, has me pinned hard against the side of the barn, and will *not* let me go. What would you do?

After a while it "dawns on me" to give him a scratch behind his ears, as I often did when we were not wrestling. Guess what? He let me go. Besides, he might realize that he would now win every match easily that he ever had with me again, which he did, and let me go each time with a scratch behind his ears.

We remained friends for as long as he lived, meaning that my dad insisted eventually on butchering him for meat we needed for the freezer. I refused to eat him for a long time, until I finally decided it was a way of allowing him to live inside me, which some might say he still does. Consider our Native American history (After all, my great-grandmother was a full-blooded American Indian). Consider also traditional Buffalo hunts of the sort you see in *Dances with Wolves*.

Political wrestling can easily get carried away, and politicians often don't have the Good Sense of my young bull friend. Politicians seem to prefer to get you against the wall and Obstruct/Resist you to your death. That is why I think that young bull was much wiser than many politicians. I won't speak for older bulls of course, but this one wanted to be my friend as long as he lived.

Of course this is too simple a solution for politics, or is it? Another "dirt stick" type, Abraham Lincoln, once said: "A drop of honey draws more flies than a gallon of gall." In our political world today we have used so many gallons of gall that it is downright unhealthy for today's political Embodiment. What are we doing about this?

Consider Mohammed bin Abdul Karim al Isaa, Secretary General of the Muslim World League, who reminded Muslims not long ago concerning their relations with Jews: "A neighbor of the Prophet (Muhammed) was a Jew, and when the Jew was ill, the Prophet visited him and gave him kind words". Since then President Trump achieved the new peace agreement between Israel and most Muslim countries except for Iran.

Welcome to the Political Pig-Wallow. As my grandma, not my mom of course, always told me: "A little dirt never hurt anybody". We are all just hogs when it comes right down to it. However, I am not only a pig but a nice person when you get to know me.

The Populist Movement had the right idea, whether you agree with their politics or not. It began with conversations across diverse cultural, religious, racial, sexual, and even political lines.

Unfortunately Populism has allowed itself often to be sucked into polarized territory. Political Parties and Populists may need to extend their methods to incorporate even newer kinds of friends today, not just reinforce themselves with friends they already have.

In the neck of the woods where I grew up, men gathered at Fair's Lunch for a "wet tenderloin" sandwich and/or "chili bowl" and after that a game of pool in the back room. There, no matter who wins, they sit down again, have a beer or whatever, shake hands, and head back to work or wherever, often with their arms around each other's shoulders. I don't think they were of the same religion or whatever, even the same political party.

I was only a kid, but I have never forgotten this, and still think of that as the American Spirit. What has gone wrong with us?

I am an American and like to think Americans love each other. I admit that I have to stretch myself a bit, but I need to *Believe* in this in the sense of "*Have Confidence In*". It is more important to be *Americans* than which side of a political battle we are on.

You and I need to reach out to strangers, not to win a fight, but to consolidate the notoriously Polarized sides of the American Body Politic.

So reach out not just to win over new warriors but to consolidate a *real Communitas*. Reach out in whatever ways "dawn on you". When you take to someone to lunch or whatever, *don't* start with politics. Start with something that reminds you that you are or could be friends. I am not a Quaker, but I love the way they consider everybody *Friends*.

When it comes to politics, don't enter an unnecessary argument. When someone mentions their position about politics, start by saying: "I understand how (or why) you feel that way" and see if you can remain Friends by the time your conversation is over.

The only *exception* here, sadly, is *not* to invite or expect much from known Ideologist types. They are only able to talk to themselves or people exactly like them. They are only good at brainwashing, not listening to, anybody else, which is always obvious to everybody but them. They will never hear a single word you are saying, no matter what you say.

You on the other hand can have disagreements and still be friends with everybody else, even me, but not Ideots. Ask your Neurons. They have disagreements all the time and still vote for Embodiment. The living neurons live long enough to discard the already dead ones.

If we don't manage to survive the current polarization clashes, the American Spirit is gone. A new book that just came out by Ben Shapiro, *How to Destroy America in Three Steps* listed in Recommended Books. He contrasts Disintegration methods against historically basic American Unionist doctrines and quotations. He ends with a courageous but uncertain forecast.

My personal *Confidence* as described in the ethics of Part 3, Scene 4, describes *not* the past two and a half century Doctrines but sources that begin long before that in Nature itself and still Make Sense as opposed to Disintegration notions that make no sense at all because they only know how to produce Destructive results and violent riots. Like the No Culture movement, they only go Nowhere that produces anything but Destructive Results.

After all, don't you prefer to be part of a Living and Embodied Body Politic that has a long record of learning how to work through its failures to become the country envied by every country in the world who wants to move here.

PART 4
SCENE 5 RELIGIOUS APPLICATIONS: LIFE IS MORE THAN TIME OR SPACE CAN TEACH US.

How can Religion and/or God survive in our complex world today? Part 3, Scene 5 describes Nassim Taleb's Ritual and C. S. Peirce's Pragmatic approaches, in both cases focusing on *Experience that precedes Thought*. A third and similar approach is Maurice Merleau-Ponty's. His may sound Complex at first, but its basic Elements are Simple.

First, the Complex part: Merleau-Ponty goes from his famous descriptions of *Perception* to its *Origin* in what he calls the *Chiasm of Dynamic Intertwining of Polarities* at the center of which is what philosophers traditionally call *Being*.

Subject and Object, Inside and Outside, Time and Space, Visible and Invisible, etc. are among Polarities used to *Describe* how things operate, and polar possibilities are never-ending. *Reversibility of Polarities means that neither side of any polarities has definable meaning Except as the Opposite of the Other. There is Nothing between them.*

Second, the Simple part: *Merleau-Ponty has a Simple question: What are they really Defining when Polarities all by themselves describe Nothing about what anything Is? Merleau-Ponty's second Simple question is: What, if anything, holds Polarities together, which is Nothing, as Reversibility shows.*

His Elemental answer to both questions is: The Nothing that is supposedly between them is more than Nothing. Although they may be Indefinable, these things are obviously Here and Now. Can anyone experience anything otherwise?

Your Elemental Experience lets you know Elementally that you are not only Here and Now, despite your indefinability, you are not an inanimate object. You are Alive, which is another Elemental. You are Alive, and although every day you are different, you are still the same person with the same name, right?

I may be paraphrasing Merleau-Ponty a bit, but this is what I believe he is saying. This Life therefore makes You an absolutely Unique human being, agreed? That is a simple Elemental truth.

For me personally this goes back to my childhood and what was taught to me even before I met Oral Hildebrand: *"Life is more than clocks and maps can teach us"*, which my Grandmother taught me. I just upgraded it a bit for this Scene subtitle in order to fit what Merleau-Ponty describes in his book *Visible and Invisible*.

Merleau-Ponty uses as his source the poet Paul Claudel, and for all I know Claudel may also have been mimicking his own childhood.

In my childhood we inherently granted that despite the fact that we could never "Prove" things are really Here and Now is that we simply and safely "Assume" it because anyone with basic common sense Experiences things that way. In other words, the only real Test for this is Simply that we all or nearly all naturally agree. Polarities may help us in many ways to describe things, but they can also leave a lot out, no matter how many Polarities they use.

So all of this is Really very Simple when it comes right down to it. Any child understands this who does not become lost in Polarities and forget that we are both Here (Space) and Now (Time) because we all Experience things that way.

It is unfortunate that today's urban society raises children without such *Elemental* and *Pragmatic Knowledge*. To me this reflects on the childhood ethical problems Kristeva describes in Part 4 Scene 2. And it is also quite consistent with Peirce and Taleb. *Everything begins in contact with the Origins of Experience, not thoughts that come along later. We already know this by then.*

Polar opposites always ignore momentarily what Merleau-Ponty calls *Elementals* (in his early works he calls them Primary Processes, Elementary States, etc.).

In us humans he calls this Flesh, which is like all Elementals and ultimately Indefinable in Polar terms because, like all Elementals, Flesh Precedes polar terminology, yet is obviously Present because We are all Obviously Here in the Flesh and Experience it.

Flesh is quite different from Meat in a cute science fiction story about extraterrestrials who visit Earth and discover that humans are made of Meat. They leave our planet quickly because they cannot imagine how Meat could possibly be a source of Intelligence. Take a look at hamburger and you can see why they would say this.

They should have read Merleau-Ponty while they were here. Meat is easy to define with polar terms like This as opposed to That, etc. *Flesh* is in itself *impossible even with polarities*. Merleau-Ponty uses Flesh because it was the first term scientists used for our "insides", *before* they started dissecting with polar terming like *this* as opposed to *that*, etc., then forgot *what* they were dissecting and went on to describe everything in polar terms *as if this includes everything*.

Flesh as Elemental therefore describes humans as "*Singular without a Plural*", which is exactly True. We are all Flesh, so we as individuals are unexplainably *Unique*. In ordinary language, there is nobody like You on the face of the earth. *Elementary*, as Sherlock Holmes would say.

Scientists have been trying for a long time to explain where your consciousness, for example, is located within your brain and/or body and never found *where* exactly you *are*. You may be in an *outdoor location*, but where you are *inside* your body is Indefinable except Elementally, which is to say that You are obviously *Here* and *Now*, wherever or whenever, right?

Merleau-Ponty loves to describe what appear to be *Simple* things that we usually ignore. When your finger touches an object, it is one Sensation, but when your finger touches a finger on the other hand, it is still *one* sensation, not *two*, right? *Elementary, as Sherlock Holmes would say.*

Now, what does all this have to do with Religion and/or God? *Flesh, Elemental, Chiasm, Life, and perhaps even God (for those who Experience God) all could be called Elementals.* God is the most Universal Elemental *for those who Experience God*. As Merleau-Ponty says in his earliest work, *God is Everywhere and Elsewhere.*

At long last we will finally in this book attempt to relate God to the religious world. All religions are Elemental, as you have possibly gathered already, yet they are obviously not necessarily Theistic. According to Merleau-Ponty, it goes like this:

It Makes Sense to utilize *Embodied* (*Elemental*) descriptions (Sound familiar?) to describe how God *Lives* "Betwixt and Between" Polarities, so *Life* can be described in either Elemental or Polar terms.

Elemental Life lies *between* any polarities. However, it is interesting to ask whether God is Dead or Alive in Polar terms. Is God Alive or Dead? *The best Elemental answer we can relate to* Polar *terms is Both*.

Consider another classic polarity, Subject and Object. To Merleau-Ponty recent centuries fell off in similar fashion but on opposite sides of Subject and Object poles. *Science* fell off on the *Objective* side in the 18-19th centuries because since it could not find God anywhere *outside*, so there must be no God anywhere. Philosophy and Psychology fell off on the Subjective side, as in Death of God claimed by Friedrich Nietzsche and Sigmund Freud, where God is *inside* is at best a projected Father figure.

Embodiment

In both cases to Merleau-Ponty, they miss *the middle ground* because they see only the subjective *or* objective polar sides of things and no Elemental Reality between them.

To Merleau-Ponty God Lives an Elemental Life between Polar Life and Death, in which God is in polar terms both Dead and Alive, so if God is to be found "anywhere", it is in the Elemental world of Embodiment, another Elemental.

For a start, Merleau-Ponty credits Augustine for focusing Religion on the Inward "Me" instead of Outward "Doctrines". (Both he and Augustine had rejected the Catholic Church when young because of its rigid Doctrines and its denial of the "Revolutionary Spirit".) Here Christopher Von Simpson in Recommended Books picks up Medieval Catholic Mystics and runs with them.)

Here things do become very Complex. Since *Embodiment* is an *Elemental*, it connects polarities Eternity and Time, so Christianity involves the *Incarnation (Embodiment)* of God in order to *Connect* things *Elementally*. In short, Eternity needs Time in order to provide humans with meaning, but as a philosopher rather than religion expert, that is as far as Merleau-Ponty goes before his fatal heart attack mentioned earlier.

Christianity goes much farther in its answer to such questions by interconnecting the Life and Death of Jesus that could possibly describe an Elemental Life that transcends polarities.

Other Religions actually have somewhat similar Elemental notions: Judaism in the eternal life, death, and revival of Israel, Eastern Religion in the Nothingness that is more than Nothing in inherent balancing Experiences of Life, etc. (You can find grounding for the latter in my friend Jayakumar Raghavan's book in Recommended Books.)

OMG as they say. Where do *we* go with all this? It may be somewhat easier in descriptions of religion by C. S. Peirce or Nasim Taleb in Part 3, Scene 5, because Peirce and Taleb do not venture as Merleau-Ponty does into the depths of *Embodied Incarnation*.

What do Christians themselves historically say?

First, Consider for Christians how Jesus Died on the Cross, and yet still Lives. (Judaism has somewhat similar ideas concerning the survival of Israel, Islam has survived in their Rites of Passage, etc.)

Second, it is apparent that Religion thus far has survived collectively and individually through many of Life's (in the Elemental sense) Rites of Passage, which are also full of Life and Death issues not physically but metaphorically.

Third, Christian accounts of Jesus rising from the dead are vague in polar terminology (as are Elementals generally). In The Gospel of John, Mary Magdalen is the first to see a Risen Jesus, but she doesn't even recognize him, and when she does, he tells her not to try to take hold of him. I mean, what kind of body is resurrected here?

When Merleau-Ponty gets into such things in his early works, he suggests once that Jesus' *Real* Resurrection is in his people as the Body of Christ, but for most Christians this is not going far enough, although *Elementally* if not *Biblically*, some folks think it is.Fourth, it is much easier to understand *Pragmatically* than *Objectively* the Rites of Passage in Christianity, Judaism, Islam, or Buddhism. They work in any case for many folks Elementally and/or Experientially and/or Pragmatically if not Rationally.

Fifth, consider Merleau-Ponty's notion of *Universal Pregnancy* near the end of *Visible and Invisible*, whether in Silence, Space, Perception, whatever or wherever. In *Nature* he calls this the *Offenheit of Umwelt*, the Openness and Unpredictability of Nature, i.e., Nature from bottom to top is always *Pregnant*.

I leave it to you to make sense of whatever in any of the Five above might work in terms of your own Experience.

Such processes, in any case, *always* involve *Risk*, which Nassim Taleb calls "Skin in the Game". *Talk* is cheap. *Pregnancy* is not, agreed? *Talk is Thought oriented, Pregnancy is Experience.*

This can lead to dramatic personal and/or cultural changes that in Part 3, Scene 5 are called *Transmogrifications*. The boundaries between Transmogrification and Religious Transformation are not always clear, especially when it takes over 30 years for mine thus far as described in Part 3, Scene 5. (I told you long ago I am a slow learner.)

For me this starts as an anti-religious stage but ends as a religious transformation. I am still not a member of a Christian Church, nor are many American Christians. I have explored again joining one recently but gave that up again because I don't feel "at home" there. For now I am satisfied to be a Christian without a Church except occasionally to attend, which is true for many Americans.

I did just buy a copy of Leonardo da Vinci's recently discovered painting of Jesus looking viewers directly in our eyes. My photos and paintings of Bonnie had been looking me for the last 10 years since her passing, but it was before I began hearing her speak.

So I know better than pushing this when if ever I hear Da Vinci's Jesus specifically and audibly say anything to me. However, I read recently that Medieval mystics, such as Teresa of Avila whom I quote in *Youniverse*, used such methods, and I am beginning to hear at least a little.

All of us have our own ways of how we *Participate* in things (Thanks again Arnold). We vary widely from one of us to another. Mine may strike you as somewhere between understandable and insane, but we are all Unique, right?

What most of Part 4. Scene 5 has related to Belief is the sense of "Having Confidence In" whoever or however rather than Belief in Doctrines, again as in Part 4, Scene 2. We all search for what Makes Sense to Us, so we don't have to agree with everybody about everything. Nobody has any right to say what makes sense to us *Individually* should be required of *Everybody, yet in the Spirit of the 21st Century, we need to feel Bonded with each other as Friends in a very wide way..*

Therefore, I want to make it clear that this book is not making an effort to convert readers to my version of Whatever. That depends on the Unique Singularity of what makes You feel happy or have a sense of "well being", whether you are Atheist, Humanist, Jew, Christian, Buddhist, or whatever.

Your life is yours and not anybody else's. While reading this book you may have been working through your own version of such things, however different it may be from mine. Recall my earlier reference to folks in my home town at Fair's Lunch?

If we share our Experiences with each other it is still possible that we can all be Friends, right? We don't have to agree about much of anything as long as we Participate Positively and Creatively in the development of what in these two books is called the Spirit of the Twenty-First Century, the boundaries of which are still formulating.

In time this century will result in either the Disintegration or Survival of the Living Spirit of the 21st Century, and we all Participate in this Process of either Dying Cultural Disintegration or Living Cultural Embodiment

This book therefore ends not with any persuasive rationalisms but instead a Dream of Tomorrow.

EPILOGUE

DAWN

What follows is a dream one night near the end of writing the first edition of this book:

While making rounds at a hospital, a nurse approaches from the maternity ward and asks me to come to a nearby delivery room where they are uncertain what to do with a young nurse in training who has just witnessed her first real-life child delivery.

As I enter the room, she just sits there staring into space. I approach her from the direction toward which she is staring and attempt to wave a high-five to congratulate her on her accomplishment. She stares right though me.

I move closer and get face to face with her and stare into her eyes...... until I get very dizzy...... and wake up.

My bedroom is a total mess, a pig-wallow you might say. Clothes, pillows, sheets, bedspread, shoes, socks, books, magazines, etc. are strewn in all directions. The Bipap equipment that helps me with my occasional sleep-apnea problems lies prone on the carpet.

I begin to laugh. Messy Jesse has struck again.

Then I notice that it is beginning to get light outside, something I love to watch as the sun shines through my Jungle. I walk to the slider door and see through the trees that the sun is just beginning to appear, so I open the slider and go out on the patio and look across the swimming pool at the Sunrise.

As I stand there staring, somehow I know it is going to be a good day, and I smile. This time the sun has no tears.

RECOMMENDED BOOKS

Benz, Arnold. *Astrophysics and Creation: Perceiving the Universe through Science and Participation*. Crossroads, New York, 2016.

Brown, Raymond E. *The Gospel According to John*. Doubleday, New York, 1970.

Campbell, Joseph and Henry R. Robinson. *A Skeleton Key toFinnegan's Wake: Unlocking James Joyce's Masterwork*. World Library, Novato CA, 1961.

Clark, Andy. *Mindware, An Introduction to the Philosophy of Cognitive Science*. Oxford, New York, 2014.

_____. *Surfing Uncertainty, Prediction, Action, and the Embodied Mind*. Oxford, 2015.

Connolly, William E. *A world of Becoming*. Duke, 2011.

Damasio, Antonio. *Descartes' Error: Emotion and the Human Brain*. Penguin, New York, 1994.

_. *Looking for Spinoza: Joy, Sorrow, and the Feeling Brain*. Harcourt, Orlando, 2003.

_____. *The Strange Order of Things: Life, Feeling, and the Making of Cultures*. Pantheon, New York, 2018.

Downing, Christine. *Women's Mysteries: Toward a Politics of Gender*. Spring, South Burlington VT, 1992, 2003.

Dreyfus, Hubert. *Skillful Coping: Essays on the Phenomenology of Everyday Perception and Action*. Oxford, 2014.

Eliade, Mircea. *Rites and Symbols, Mysteries of Birth and Rebirth*.

Spring, South Burlington, VT, 1984.

Ellmann, Richard. *James Joyce: New and Revised Edition*. Oxford, 1982.

Finlay, B. Bret and Marie-Claire Arietta. *Let them Eat Dirt: Saving your Child from an Over-Sanitized World*. Algonquin Books, Chapel Hill NC, 2017.

Freeman, Walter. *Societies of Brains, The Neurobiology of Love and Hate*. Lawrence Erlbaum, Mahwah, NJ, 1995.

_____. *How Brains Make Up Their Minds*, Columbia, 2000.

Hausman, Carl. *Charles S. Peirce's Evolutionary Philosophy*. Cambridge, UK, 1994.

Hilton, Steve. *More Human, Designing a World where People Come First*. Perseus, New York, 2016.

Hookway, Christopher. *Peirce*. Routledge, London, 1985.

Gell-Mann, Murray. *The Quark and the Jaguar, Adventures in the Simple and the Complex*. Henry Holt and Co., New York 1994.

Kauffman, Stuart. *Reinventing the Sacred: A New View of Science,*

Reason and Religion. Basic Books, New York, 2008.

_____. *Humanity in a Creative Universe*. Oxford, 2016.

Kearney, Richard and Jens Zinnermann, eds. *Reimaging the Sacred*. Columbia, New York, 2016.

Lawler, Leonard. *Implications of Immanence, Toward a New Concept of Life*. Fordham, New York, 2006.

_____ . *Thinking Through French Philosophy, The Being of the Question*. Bloomington, IN, Indiana, 2003.

Merleau-Ponty, Maurice. *Phenomenology of Perception*. Routledge London, 1966.

_____.*The Visible and Invisible*. Northwestern, Evanston, 1968.

_____. *Sense an Nonsense*. Northwestern UP, Evanston , 1964.

Misak, Cheryl. *The Cambridge Companion to Peirce*. Cambridge UK, 2004.

_____. *Truth and the End of Inquiry: A Peircian Account of Truth*.

Clarendon-Oxford, 2004.

Mitchell, Melanie. *Complexity: A Guided Tour*. Oxford, 2o09.

_____. *Artificial Intelligence: A Guide for Thinking Humans*. Farrar, Straus, New York, 2019.

Peirce, Charles S. *Chance, Love, and Logic: Philosophical Essays*. Harcourt Brace, New York, 1923. (2015 reprint available on Amazon.)

_____. *C. S. Peirce: The Essential Writing*, Ed., E. C. Moore.

Prometheus, New York, 1998.

Raghavan, Jayakumar. *Science for Living, 5 Science Topics for Religion and Society*. Novinka, New York, 2015.

Raybold, Arthur. *Home from the Banks, Poems*. Wigeon Publishing, Sand Diego, 2012.

Sapolsky, Robert. *Behave: The Biology of Humans at Our Best and Worst*, Penguin Press, 2017.

Shapiro, Ben. *How to Destroy America in Three Easy Steps*. Broadside Books, New York, 2020.

Simpson, Christopher Von. *Merleau-Ponty and Theology*. Bloomsbury, London, 2013.

Schechner, Richard. *Between Theater and Anthropology*. University of Pennsylvania, 1985.

Slovic, Paul. *The Feeling of Risk., New Perspectives on Risk Perception*. Routledge, 2015.

Slovic, Scott and Paul Slovic. *Numbers and Nerves, Information, Emotion, and Meaning*. Oregon State Press, 2015.

Sowell, Thomas. *Charter Schools and their Enemies*. Basic Books,

New York, 202o.

 Taleb, Nassim, *Antifragility: The Impact of the Highly Improbable*. Random House, New York, 2010.

_____. *Skin in the Game: Hidden Asymmetries in Daily Life*, Random House, New York, 2018.

Taylor, Charles. *Sources of Self: The Making of Modern Identity*. Harvard UP, Cambridge, 1989.

_____. *A Secular Age*. Harvard, 2007

Thelen, Esther and Linda Smith. *Dynamic Systems: Approach to the Development of Cognition and Action*. MIT, Cambridge, 1996.

Thomas, Jesse J. *The Youniverse: The Spirit of the 21st Century*, Fifth Edition. GoT0Publish, Atlanta, 2020.

_____. *Embodiment, How Animals and Humans Make Sense of Things: The Dawn of Art, Ethics, Science, Politics, and Religion*, 2020 Edition. GoToPublish, Atlanta, 2020.

Turner, Victor. *The Ritual Process: Structure and Anti-Structure*.

Aldine Transaction, New Brunswick, 1969, 1997.

Waddington, C. H. *The Strategy of Genes*. Routledge, New York, 1957, 2014.

www.ingramcontent.com/pod-product-compliance
Lightning Source LLC
LaVergne TN
LVHW091538060526
838200LV00036B/664